JAPAN'S PUBLIC POLICY COMPANIES

AEI-Hoover
policy studies

The studies in this series are issued jointly
by the American Enterprise Institute
for Public Policy Research and the Hoover
Institution on War, Revolution and Peace.
They are designed to focus on
policy problems of current and future interest,
to set forth the factors underlying
these problems and to evaluate
courses of action available to policy makers.
The views expressed in these studies
are those of the authors and do not necessarily
reflect the views of the staff, officers,
or members of the governing boards of
AEI or the Hoover Institution.

JAPAN'S
PUBLIC POLICY
COMPANIES

Chalmers Johnson

HD
3616
$.J33$
$J64$

American Enterprise Institute for Public Policy Research
Washington, D.C.

Hoover Institution on War, Revolution and Peace
Stanford University, Stanford, California

AEI-Hoover policy studies 24

Library of Congress Cataloging in Publication Data

Johnson, Chalmers A.
    Japan's public policy companies.

    (AEI-Hoover policy studies; 24) (Hoover Institution studies; 60)
    Includes index.
    1. Industry and state—Japan.   2. Corporations—Japan.
    3. Japan—Economic policy—1945–
I. Title.   II. Series.   III. Series:
Hoover Institution studies; 60.
HD3616.J33J64   338.952   77-28020
ISBN 0-8447-3272-9

Printed in the United States of America

Contents

Preface

The many attempts by governments here and abroad to influence the workings of their market economies have consequences both intended and unintended. The relationship between governments and economies thus is a matter of intense public controversy, as well as a primary source of research topics for analysts of public policy; and Japan looms large in the debates. Japan's official pressures on the market are comparatively heavy in some respects (protectionism, indicative planning, administrative guidance) and light in others (tax burden, welfare); at the same time, Japan has recorded levels of economic performance that exceed those of any other bureaucratically skewed economy. Some analysts employ the concept of "Japan, Inc." in trying to account for the success of the government-business nexus in Japan. Others hotly contend that Japan is no different from any other market economy; it is only the beneficiary of temporarily favorable conditions.

In this study I have attempted to contribute to the analysis of the Japanese case by surveying an important but relatively unknown sector of Japan's official economic bureaucracy—the public corporations and mixed public-private enterprises. I do not deal with all of the interesting aspects of Japanese governmental intervention in the economy (these broader concerns are reserved for a larger work in progress on the history of the Ministry of International Trade and Industry); nor do I believe that this book is an appropriate introduction for a novice to the Japanese political economy. This study has three aims. It is intended to bring to the attention of foreign analysts the significance of public corporate institutions in Japan; it identifies a historical dimension that has been overlooked in many attempts to explain the Japanese government-business relationship; and it stresses the influence of bureaucratic interests on the institutions of economic administration in Japan and elsewhere.

1

A note on certain Japanological problems is necessary before turning to the subject matter proper. Japanese personal names are given in the Japanese order, surname followed by given name. Readers who do not know Japanese may be irritated by the frequent use of Japanese words and titles in romanization; if so, I apologize for the necessity to include such details. However, the citation of Japanese equivalents is critical to this study for several reasons. First, the technical language of bureaucracy and administration in Japan, as in all modern countries, is invariably characterized by euphemism and disguise. An entire treatise could be written on the use of the term *chōsei* (coordination, but with overtones of control) in official titles. For Japanese bureaucratic organizations to be understandable to the outsider, their technical terms must be explicated and translated (imagine for a moment attempting to put into fully nuanced Japanese the English term "affirmative action," "underachiever," or "senior citizen"). Second, many Japanese public corporations have adopted official English titles that are not exact translations of their official Japanese titles—for instance, Institute of Developing Economies for Ajia Keizai Kenkyūjo (literally, Asian Economic Research Institute), a special legal entity under the control of the Ministry of International Trade and Industry. The Japanese title of a public corporation often conveys information that is omitted in its English title. Third, the Japanese make many distinctions that cannot be accommodated in English. For example, *kōsha, kōdan, eidan,* and *jigyōdan* are all types of public corporations for which English has no directly equivalent terms; there is no alternative but to use the Japanese words. This problem comes up in many areas of Japanese public administration. The English words "council" or "committee" may be rendered in Japanese as *shingikai, kyōgikai, shinsakai, chōsakai, kondankai, kaigi,* and *iinkai,* but these terms have very different connotations and, in some cases, different legal meanings. *Shingikai,* for example, are organs of the state under article 8 of the National Administration Organization Law, and they must be composed of "persons of learning and experience," whereas *kyōgikai* consist of representatives of an official agency and a private organization for purposes of "coordinating views" (compare the Industrial Structure Council, Sangyō Kōzō Shingikai, and the Central Social Insurance and Medical Care Council, Chūō Shakai Hoken Iryō Kyōgikai.)[1]

In this book I have used official or dictionary translations wherever possible, but for the reasons given above I have also listed Japanese

---

[1] See Kojima Kazuo (staff member of the Legislation Bureau, House of Councillors), *Hōrei ruiji yōgo jiten, magirawashii yōgo no yomikata tsukaikata* [Dictionary of similar legal terms: the reading and usage of ambiguous terminology] (Tokyo: Gyōsei K.K., 1975), pp. 171-74.

equivalents for those who are curious about what is being translated. There is one exception to this general rule. In speaking of ministries and other official agencies I render *kyoku, bu,* and *ka* as bureau, department, and section respectively, rather than the official bureau, department, and division. The glossary at the front of the book is intended to serve as a handy reference for specialized terms.

I would like to acknowledge the financial support of my research by the Center for Japanese and Korean Studies at the University of California, Berkeley. My greatest debt is to Yutani Eiji, Japanese acquisitions librarian of the East Asiatic Library at Berkeley, who has been unstinting in his efforts to collect significant materials on the Japanese official bureaucracy and economy.

CHALMERS JOHNSON
Berkeley, California
June 1977

Glossary of Japanese Terms

Japanese	Translation	Meaning
amakudari	descent from heaven	The practice of employing retired government officials as chief executives or members of boards of directors of public and private corporations.
eidan	corporation	Prewar and wartime form of *kōdan*.
gaikaku dantai	auxiliary organ	Semiprivate organization(s) attached to a ministry of the central government; commonly organized as a foundation and partially staffed by active-duty government officials. (Not a *tokushu hōjin*.)
jigyōdan	enterprise unit	Government corporation(s) used to promote economic or social policies other than public works. Smaller and with less entrepreneurial freedom than *kōdan*.
kabushiki kaisha	joint stock company	Private, profit-making (that is, nongovernmental) corporation(s) created under the Commercial Code. Abbreviated K.K.
kikin	fund	One or more funds, foundations, or endowments created by law and financed partly or wholly from the national treasury.

5

Japanese	Translation	Meaning
kinko	depository	Public finance corporation(s) serving commercial and agricultural cooperatives.
kōdan	public unit	Wholly or partially government-owned corporation(s) charged with investing large-scale social overhead capital (usually public works).
kōkigyō	public enterprise	General term for public corporation(s) and mixed public-private enterprise(s).
kōko	public finance corporation	Wholly government-owned, policy-oriented finance corporation(s). Accounts submitted to the Diet.
kokusaku kaisha	national policy company	General term, in common use before World War II, to designate mixed public-private enterprise(s). See *tokushu kaisha*.
kōsha	public corporation	Wholly government-owned public corporation(s) with the strongest public character of all *tokushu hōjin*. Normally engaged in monopoly business. Budgets subject to Diet approval.
seifu kigyō	government enterprise	Agency(s) of the government directly performing industrial and commercial activities.
shadan hōjin	corporation	Incorporated private association(s) (for example, a trade association) created under the Civil Code.
shikin un'yōbu	Investment Funds Account	The name from 1951 to the present of private savings deposited in government accounts and used by the Ministry of Finance to make loans to the public corporations.
shingikai	deliberation council	Advisory organ(s), created by law and composed in part of civilians, to consult with and advise the ministries of the central government.

6

Japanese	Translation	Meaning
tokushu ginkō	special bank	Wholly government-owned bank(s), with greater entrepreneurial autonomy than *kōko*.
tokushu hōjin	special legal entity	Term used by the central government for public corporation(s) and mixed public-private enterprise(s), as distinguished from privately owned business firm(s).
tokushu kaisha	special company	Mixed public-private enterprise(s) created by law to further economic development or to protect national interests. Organized as *kabushiki kaisha*.
yokinbu	Deposits Account	The name prior to 1951 for private savings held in trust by the Ministry of Finance and used to finance public corporations.
zaidan hōjin	foundation	Nonprofit, incorporated foundation(s) created under the Civil Code.
zaikai	business world	General term used to refer collectively to the leaders of big business and finance.
zaisei tōyūshi keikaku	Fiscal Investment and Loan Plan	The second, or "investment," budget administered by the Ministry of Finance and used to finance the public corporations. Abbreviated FILP.

1
Orientations: The Japanese Government and Economy

Any society's basic institutions and processes have both open and closed, overt and covert aspects. That is, every society presents one face to the world, while maintaining its own not necessarily secret but certainly private way of getting its work done. A fundamental task of modern social scientists in explaining social phenomena is to penetrate behind the formal, external face of institutions to their practical, day-to-day workings. This is not to say that the substantive is more real than the formal; rather, social science wishes to reveal and analyze the gap between the formal and the substantive. Studying the nature and extent of the distinction between the outer and the inner, between the formal and the substantive, informs and provides intellectual excitement for innumerable social science projects, whether the topic be the way a constitution is interpreted by the courts, the way a "power elite" actually runs a community, or the discrepancy between a governmental policy and its actual effects.

Social scientists do not presume that the formal rules of a nation or an institution are misleading, only that they are superficial. If one is interested in how Americans govern themselves, it is not a mistake to begin by reading the United States Constitution; but it would leave a lot unexplained—although not necessarily misunderstood—to do nothing more than that. In contrast, the fascinating problem of the study of modern Japanese government (and a source of its considerable intellectual attraction) is the fact that the formal and overt aspects of its institutions *are* misleading as guides to how the society actually works.

The Japanese themselves are quite aware of this discrepancy and have invented terms and modes of expression to discuss it among themselves. Katō Eiichi of the Ministry of Home Affairs argues, "The

9

Japanese don't care if there is a gap between *tatemae* ("a principle," "a policy," "a rule") and reality. The Japanese are used to having foreign rules. They themselves are poor theorists, so they don't change the rules. Instead, they say 'Theory is so, but . . . ' [or] '*Tatemae* is so, but . . . ' and thus make everything possible." When a citizen appeals to the government for relief from some crisis or burden and is told by the bureaucracy that the law does not cover his case, the citizen then appeals through the newspapers or politicians. "They all cry, '*Hōritsu no kaishaku wa tomokaku* (whatever the wording of the law may be), do something good for him.' And the bureaucrats discover a new interpretation of the [usually very vague legal] definition." [1]

Amaya Naohiro, a senior official and perhaps the best known spokesman of Japan's Ministry of International Trade and Industry (MITI), distinguishes what he calls *uchiwa* ("within one's own house," "private") societies such as Japan and the contract societies of Europe. He continually invokes the term *uchiwa* to explain the relationship between his very powerful ministry and the Japanese business community, asserting that whatever the relationship looks like from the outside, *uchiwa* the relationship works. In Amaya's view, this inner understanding among the Japanese people of the tasks confronting them was the basic precondition for Japan's spectacular postwar economic growth. [2]

The Japanese public-private dichotomy poses a problem for comparative analysis that has long confronted the best foreign analysts of Japan. Dan Henderson, for example, writes:

Terms such as 'competition,' 'private industry,' or 'free enterprise,' commonly used in discussions of Japanese business, conjure up in the minds of readers in English quite different images from existing realities of Japanese business. . . . 'Collusive rivalry,' 'semiprivate industry,' 'quasi-public enterprise,' respectively, might be more apt expressions, precisely because their western referents are unclear. [3]

Henderson's point is to warn the uninitiated against drawing conclusions about how the Japanese economy works on the basis of superficial comparisons with their own societies. However, still another type of mistake often is made by foreigners who discover for themselves

---

[1] Katō Eiichi, *The Japanese Government Group Training Course in Local Government* (Tokyo: Ministry of Home Affairs, 1974), pp. 17, 19.

[2] Amaya Naohiro, *Hyōryū suru Nihon keizai* [The Japanese economy adrift] (Tokyo: Mainichi Shimbunsha, 1975), pp. 18-20.

[3] Dan F. Henderson, *Foreign Enterprise in Japan: Laws and Policies* (Tokyo: Tuttle, 1975), p. 98.

that there is a considerable difference between overt and *uchiwa* Japan. They are likely to be drawn to the large body of writing in English that argues that the Japanese are literally incomparable, that Japan's culture and historical experiences are so unlike anything else on earth that the people and their society must be unique.

It is true that Japanese cultural and historical experience is unique, and it colors modern Japanese political and economic life. But to elevate this heritage into an intellectual construct called "national character" and to use it to explain virtually all differences between Japan and other open, advanced industrial societies is both tautological —since no one knows precisely what national character is—and unprofitable, since it precludes making the kinds of serious comparisons that will reveal the genuine strengths and weaknesses of Japanese institutions. Conversely, to deny that there is much difference between Japan's and, say, the political economy of the United States is simply uninformed, given the cultural and historical differences between the two countries.[4]

Why, then, is the formal structure of Japanese institutions a poor guide to how the Japanese political economy actually works? The main reason seems to be, as Katō Eiichi indicates, that most of these institutions are borrowings from abroad. Foreign institutions, such as parliaments, corporations, and public enterprises, have had and continue to have a major influence in Japan; but the external observer will be misled if he presumes that these forms work the same way that they do—or are thought to do—in the countries from which they were borrowed.

To put the matter in somewhat more theoretical terms, the Japanese have applied existing institutional structures to meet their own functional needs. The distinction in social science between structure and function has been used most commonly to explain structural variability, not functional variability. Analysts who employ structural-functional theory in its many forms are usually concerned with how a particular society fulfills some universal functional need with a structure that is uncommon or that may not be found in any other society. The concern in this study, however, is the opposite. It is to show how a structure that is quite common in all open, industrialized societies—the public corpora-

---

[4] For examples of studies that take these two views, respectively, see Herman Kahn, *The Emerging Japanese Superstate* (Englewood Cliffs, N. J.: Prentice-Hall, 1970); and Hugh Patrick and Henry Rosovsky, eds., *Asia's New Giant: How the Japanese Economy Works* (Washington, D.C.: Brookings Institution, 1976).

tion and the mixed public-private enterprise—functions quite differently in Japan from the way it does in most comparable societies.[5]

The distinction is an important one. Most people find it easy to perceive that different structures may perform the same functions in different societies. (Some believe this too easily, such as visitors to totalitarian societies who assume that Communist parties or institutionalized dictators are the same things as parliaments and presidents.) However, people often are disturbed, even irritated and suspicious, when they encounter structures—parliaments, bureaucracies, public corporations—that function differently from those with which they are familiar. It is an understandable confusion, particularly if the structures bear the same names, in translation, as the names of structures in their own societies and were in fact derived from them: compare, for example, the differing functions of formal, written constitutions in the United States and in Japan. Anyone who has studied the literature on Japanese politics and foreign relations will recognize the problem.

Contrast with the West

In this book I am concerned with how the Japanese public enterprises came into being, are financed, and serve diverse public—and sometimes not so public—purposes. These enterprises are numerous—estimates range from over a hundred to several thousand, depending on the definitions and criteria used. Some function like their equivalents in Western Europe and North America, but most do not.

In pointing out that Japanese public enterprises differ from those of the West, even though they are still called public enterprises, I do not mean to suggest that Japanese enterprises ought to change to a Western pattern, or that there is some trickery on the part of the Japanese in providing new functions for old structures. American political leaders and editorial writers inevitably become irritated, for

---

[5] J. P. Nettl illustrates this point neatly in an Anglo-French context: "In France, the successful extension of the spirit of *planification* since 1945 has drawn a whole series of individuals and institutional representatives from industry, the trade unions, local government, and so on, into *ad hoc* state advisory bodies; in both their function and their role these act as emanations of the state and have thus been incorporated in what has been a rapidly growing area of the state's sectoral concerns. In Britain, however—in spite of the very large extension of governmental initiatives—the independence of the advisory or consultative bodies has remained largely untouched. These bodies speak for themselves or their interests; they are not state organizations, and *consequently* the function—and above all the role—of governmental agencies in decision-making continues largely as a negotiating and conflict-resolving rather than an initiating and autonomous one" ("The State as a Conceptual Variable," *World Politics*, vol. 20, no. 4 [July 1969], p. 583).

example, when they confront the apparent paradox of the Japan External Trade Organization (JETRO). An example of what the Japanese press routinely calls a "semigovernmental body," JETRO is staffed by active-duty officials of MITI, is wholly funded by the Japanese government, and is in fact a major operating arm of official Japanese trade and industrial administration. Many Americans believe that it should be clearly labelled an agency of the government and are skeptical of its "semiprivate" status.[6] My purpose is not to feed such suspicions but rather to explain how Japanese political history and bureaucratic practice make it reasonable for an organization like JETRO to be considered a public enterprise in Japan.

Japanese public corporations seem to me a useful vehicle for exploring the whole question of structural similarity and functional diversity— a question encountered in numerous other contexts in Japan, such as trade unions, the banking system, the civil service system, the welfare system, and so forth, and one that remains the major conceptual challenge for Westerners attempting to analyze Japanese government and politics. But the subject of public corporations is also important in its own right. There are techniques, both positive and negative, that foreigners can learn from the Japanese. The Japanese use the public corporate form in ways other open societies do not, though they also use it in the same way all open industrial societies do (for instance, to control natural monopolies, to raise revenue). Japan's unusual uses are instructive because all industrialized societies currently are faced with a series of new issues that demand public responses and policies, and for which the Japanese appear to have some answers. Yet it is remarkable how often the same writers who note that the Japanese have borrowed extensively from other societies to create their unique institutions do not imagine that other societies could find anything to borrow from Japan.

Japan's use of the public corporate form seems especially likely to be informative to Westerners because so many current problems, such as developing new energy supplies, controlling environmental damage, phasing in various new technologies and phasing out old ones, using land rationally, and maintaining a citizen's income during retirement, require governmental solutions. Even if people were not demanding that their governments address these issues, governments probably would have to become involved in them anyway, given the risks and amounts of capital most of the issues entail. The only unit of society that commands the resources and can accept the risks of major technological innovation in our "post-industrial society" is the government.

---

[6] See, for example, "Japanese Case: How Foreign Lobby Molds U.S. Opinion," *San Francisco Chronicle,* September 15, 1976 (reprinted from *Washington Post*).

13

In societies such as Great Britain and the United States, virtually every solution that has been imagined to most of the problems of advanced industrial societies involves an expansion of the official bureaucracy. Yet this consequence has often overwhelmed and destroyed the very solution it was intended to implement. By contrast, the Japanese government spends less but seems to get more for its money than comparable governments elsewhere, even though it plays a very active role in all phases of economic life. Table 1 details certain useful comparisons between Japan and other open political economies in 1959 —a useful benchmark year during Japan's high-speed growth and before

Table 1
RELATIVE WEIGHT OF THE PUBLIC ECONOMIC SECTOR
IN ELEVEN OPEN POLITICAL ECONOMIES (1959)

	Govt. Income as % of GNP	Public Enterprises' Fixed Capital Formation as % of All Fixed Capital Formation	Public Enterprises' Work Force as % of Work Force in All Enterprises
Civil free enterprise economy			
United States	28	4	2
Japan	20	11	6
Belgium	23	11	4
Middle-of-the-road economy			
West Germany	35	17	8
Netherlands	32	15	7
Sweden	30	17	8
Norway	—	15	10
Mixed public-private economy			
Austria	36	33	16·
Italy	29	30	15
France	32	38	14
United Kingdom	31	35	16

Source: Katō Hiroshi, ed., *Nihon no kōkigyō* [Japan's public enterprises] (Tokyo: Nihon Keizai Shimbunsha, 1968), p. 24.

government began to relax its controls over the economy. Table 2 reports comparisons by the Organization for Economic Cooperation and Development (OECD) among its member countries on governmental expenditure and revenue as a percentage of gross national product in 1971.

Table 2
GOVERNMENT EXPENDITURE AND REVENUE
IN OECD MEMBER COUNTRIES
(percent of GNP)

	Current Expenditure	Current Revenue
Australia[a]	22.5	28.9
Austria[b]	29.9	35.9
Belgium[a]	33.4	35.2
Canada[a]	33.7	36.3
Denmark[c]	31.4	37.5
Finland[a]	29.3	38.0
France[b]	32.5	37.2
Germany[a]	32.9	38.4
Greece[c]	23.6	27.2
Iceland[d]	25.3	33.8
Ireland[a]	32.3	33.6
Italy[a]	34.3	33.5
Japan[b]	14.3	21.9
Luxembourg[d]	33.2	34.8
Netherlands[b]	39.0	44.1
Norway[a]	40.1	47.8
Spain[a]	18.6	22.6
Sweden[a]	40.0	49.1
Switzerland[c]	21.7	26.5
United Kingdom[b]	31.9	39.7
United States[a]	30.7	30.3

Source: The OECD Member Countries (Paris: Organization for Economic Cooperation and Development, 1973).
[a] 1971 data.
[b] 1970 data.
[c] 1969 data.
[d] 1968 data.

15

This is not to say that Japanese public corporations are close to perfect, or that they ought to be copied abroad. Many Japanese analysts believe that their corporations are much less efficient than some of those in Western Europe, and they are quite critical of the use of corporations as extensions of the overt bureaucracy, as lucrative retirement spots for government officials, and as possible breeding grounds for corrupt relations between government and business. Yet they note that most areas of technological expertise in which Japan is preeminent—shipbuilding, railroads, steel, electronics, cameras—were developed by mixed public-private enterprises or under official auspices. The point is simply that Japanese public corporations are worthwhile for Westerners to study in their own right, as major institutions used by the second-largest open industrial society for getting its public work done. Particularly for those of us in other societies who are concerned that no matter how much money is spent, the public work is not getting done, or it is being done inefficiently or corruptly, a comparison with Japanese institutions can be most useful.

Functions of Japanese Public Corporations

Public enterprises in Japan perform many different functions. For one, they make loans to implement official industrial policies and to aid low productivity or declining sectors of the economy. They also spend funds to strengthen the industrial infrastructure or to develop resources. They help stabilize prices; they produce revenue; and they do research. My greatest concern in this study is the role of public corporations as a medium of governmental influence in and over the total economy, although I shall touch on and illustrate the entire range of functions. Public corporations are only one medium of governmental influence: others include direct governmental licensing and approval of private economic activities, extensive consultation between the government and the private sector, so-called administrative guidance of the economy by the government, informal public-private interconnections through retired government officials who become executives for profit-making corporations, and other old-boy networks.[7] But government corporations and mixed public-private enterprises are a critical part of what is called the government-business relationship in Japan.

---

[7] See, inter alia, Chalmers Johnson, "The Reemployment of Retired Government Bureaucrats in Japanese Big Business," *Asian Survey*, vol. 14, no. 11 (November 1974), pp. 953-65; and "MITI and Japanese International Economic Policy," in Robert A. Scalapino, ed., *The Foreign Policy of Modern Japan* (Berkeley and Los Angeles: University of California Press, 1977), pp. 227-79.

Among American scholars specializing in Japanese problems, considerable disagreement exists as to the nature of the Japanese government-business relationship. On the one hand, political scientists and political economists are impressed by the Japanese government's role in promoting Japanese economic growth and development, both before and after World War II. On the other hand, some economists and U.S. government officials are unimpressed: they contend that Japan's economy would not look very different if the government had not taken a hand, and they suggest that the government-business connection in Japan does not differ in essentials from that in other open, industrial societies.

Illustrating the first point of view is a comparative study of the modernization of Japan and Russia, written by Cyril Black and a team of scholars. This group concludes:

> Japan's governmental economic policy has not been an innovation of the postwar period, but an effective continuation of directions taken as early as the nineteenth century. Most recently, the talented bureaucrats of the Ministry of International Trade and Industry (MITI) have been among the chief architects of the policy, and they have consistently emphasized working through the market. Central planning in Japan, such as it is, can at best be called indicative. Success has depended on a broad consensus between business leaders and government officials.... Japanese industrial policy gave the country the advantages of capitalism and socialism at the same time. Capitalism's main advantage is efficiency, which was assured by allowing competition and market forces to play their role; simultaneously, close and harmonious government and business connecticns, together with rational and integrated policies, permitted considerable political control over the growth process.... The capitalist-socialist approach has resulted in relatively logical, clear, and consistent industrial policies—and is one of the best examples of 'catch-up economics.' [8]

Another team of scholars studying the basic functioning of the Japanese economy reached the opposite conclusion. Their study's joint editors, Hugh Patrick and Henry Rosovsky, contend, "The Japanese government has never taken the lead in directly encouraging the transfer of resources away from inefficient uses; rather, this has occurred through the operations of the market place." And in an article in this study, Philip Trezise, a former official of the U.S. State Department who was directly concerned with Japanese-American economic relations,

[8] Cyril E. Black et al., *The Modernization of Japan and Russia* (New York: Free Press, 1975), pp. 287-88.

17

writes, "Economic growth was a ranking objective in this society, but the particulars of the process were not willed or foreseen by anyone, politician or civil servant." [9]

One cannot help thinking that American bureaucrats who have trouble accepting what Black and his group credit the Japanese economic bureaucracy with accomplishing are skeptical because their own bureaucracy's economic accomplishments have been rather modest by comparison. More to the point, such reluctance to acknowledge the effectiveness of official Japanese industrial policy seems to be another example of people's unease when confronted by similar structures performing divergent functions. The Japanese do not employ some unknown principles of economics, as Patrick and Rosovsky suggest. However, Japanese organs of state do perform functions that differ from those assigned to the government in the United States: this Patrick and Rosovsky have both failed to study and unwittingly misinterpreted.

The second of the two views cited here brings up another problem, one of considerable importance to the credibility of much scholarship on Japan. This is the problem of inadequate, or imprecise, comparison. One of the fascinating puzzles of Japanese studies is that no agreement exists among foreign scholars—or among Japanese, for that matter—on what constitutes a proper comparative frame of reference for Japan. Thus, Japan has been compared to Russia in terms of developmental patterns; to Turkey, also in terms of development; to China, in terms of cultural orientations and responses to Western intrusion; to Bismarckian Germany, in terms of prewar state structures; and, most commonly and probably most misleadingly, to the United States, in terms of the economic and political institutions of industrial democracies. Few other societies have been assigned to so many different comparative universes.

The explanations Americans have advanced for Japan's postwar economic growth rate—the highest rate ever recorded for an industrialized society—usually come from those who believe the Japanese economy operates more or less according to the same rules as the American economy. These observers ascribe Japan's postwar growth to an unusually favorable international environment—specifically, Japan's alliance with the United States, and U.S. willingness to supply Japan with the most advanced technology at bargain-basement prices. But, comparatively speaking, this is no explanation at all. As Andrea Boltho of the OECD puts it:

Three of the countries with which Japan can most profitably be compared (France, Germany, and Italy) shared some or

---

[9] Patrick and Rosovsky, *Asia's New Giant,* pp. 46, 810-11. Note that Henry Rosovsky is a contributor to both the Black and Patrick-Rosovsky symposia.

all of Japan's initial advantages—e.g., flexible labor supplies, a very favorable (in fact even more favorable) international environment, the possibility of rebuilding an industrial structure using the most advanced techniques. Yet other conditions were very dissimilar. The most crucial difference was perhaps in the field of economic policies. Japan's government exercised a much greater degree of both intervention and protection than did any of its Western European counterparts; and this brings Japan closer to the experience of another set of countries—the centrally planned economies.[10]

Qualifications: Socialism, Origin, and Planning

It should be clear by now that my own position is close to that of Black and his colleagues, although I believe their summary view quoted earlier requires three qualifications. The first concerns their statement that "Japanese industrial policy gave the country the advantages of capitalism and socialism at the same time." Similarly, Boltho's comment compares Japan with the "centrally planned economies." Strictly speaking, socialism means social ownership of the means of production in industry and trade, and state control of the rates and directions of economic change.[11] The first criterion has never characterized Japan since the middle of the Meiji era (1868–1912); and the second criterion, while true of much of Japan's modern century, has varied enormously in extent over the century.

A second qualification to the view expressed by Black and his team has to do with when contemporary Japanese economic policy got its start. It is fairly clear that Japan's public corporations are of quite recent origin. They have existed in the domestic economy only from the founding of the Japan Iron and Steel Company in 1934, reaching their full flowering during the 1950s and 1960s. In the years immediately following the Meiji Restoration the Japanese government took the lead in introducing modern industry to Japan, creating a number of important enterprises, including mines, spinning mills, and shipyards. Government's activities during this period are an important example of direct government enterprise (*seifu kigyō*), as distinct from indirect public enterprise (*kōkigyō*), which is my primary concern in this study.

During the 1880s the government sold to private interests most of the direct enterprises it had created during the previous decade, but it never went completely out of the business of running factories and

---

[10] Andrea Boltho, *Japan: An Economic Survey 1953–1973* (London: Oxford University Press, 1975), pp. 188-89.
[11] See Benjamin N. Ward, *The Socialist Economy* (New York: Random House, 1967), p. 7.

19

installations. In 1897, the government set up the Yawata Iron and Steel Works, which it operated as a government facility until the creation of Japan Iron and Steel in 1934; and today, as we shall see, the Japanese government still operates several *seifu kigyō*.

Nonetheless, from approximately the turn of the century until the Manchurian Incident in 1931, the Japanese government's involvement in the domestic economy was minimal, compared to what developed during the 1930s and persists to the present day. In fact, the term Japanese academics generally use for intervention by the state in the private economy—"state monopoly capitalism" (*kokka dokusen shihon-shugi*)—is of quite recent origin, its Marxist flavor reflecting the prevailing ethos of the academies since the 1920s.

No Japanese scholar believes that state monopoly capitalism existed continuously from the Meiji period. Endō Shōkichi says that the Great Depression gave birth to it.[12] Fujiwara Akira and his associates contend that the financial measures government took in the wake of the Tokyo earthuake of 1923 and the financial panic of 1927 were "steps toward state monopoly capitalism," and they conclude that it actually came into being between 1929 and 1931.[13] Takahashi Makoto writes, "There [is] a variety of arguments concerning the formative period of Japan's state monopoly capitalism. The differences center on whether to date the period 1931–32 or 1936–37. The author, who attaches importance to economic control by the state by means of fiscal mechanisms, adopts the 1931–1932 theory." [14]

Thus Black and his colleagues overstate the case when they refer to the Japanese government's present economic policy as "an effective continuation of directions taken as early as the nineteenth century." Contemporary economic policy began much more recently than the nineteenth century; Meiji economic policies differ sharply from those of the Shōwa era (1926 to the present). Incidentally, "state monopoly capitalism," of which public corporations and mixed enterprises are important manifestations, is nothing more than a catch-phrase in Japan today to refer to governmental fiscal policy. It is used by people who have never read Marx, just as the term "Keynesianism" is used by Americans who have never read Keynes to mean more or less the same thing.

---

12 Endō Shōkichi, *Zaisei tōyūshi* [Fiscal investment and loan funds] (Tokyo: Iwanami Shinsho No. 595, 1966), p. 179.

13 Fujiwara Akira, Imai Seiichi, and Ōe Shinobu, eds., *Kindai Nihonshi no kiso chishiki* [Basic knowledge of modern Japanese history] (Tokyo: Yūhikaku, 1972), pp. 298, 426.

14 Takahashi Makoto, "The Development of Wartime Economic Controls," *The Developing Economies,* vol. 5, no. 4 (December 1967), p. 650, n. 2.

The third qualification to the Black statement concerns the sentence, "Central planning, such as it is, can at best be called indicative." With this remark we come face to face again with the problem with which this discussion opened—the discrepancy between Japan's superficial public face and its covert inner reality. It is quite true that official planning by the Economic Planning Agency is largely "decorative," to use Watanabe Tsunehiko's term, but a good deal of planning goes on elsewhere in the Japanese government, though it is not explicitly called planning.[15] Shiroyama Saburō, for example, holds that the Enterprises Bureau (Kigyō Kyoku, today known as the Industrial Policy Bureau, Sangyō Seisaku Kyoku) of MITI is the real "planning agency" of Japan; he believes the Economic Planning Agency serves primarily as a statistical office for it and other operating agencies of the government.[16] And the plans of the Enterprises Bureau are anything but indicative, even if, since the early 1950s, its primary means of implementation has been *yūdō kisei*, "regulation through inducement." (The word *yūdō* in Japanese actually is stronger than "inducement" in English; it is used, for example, in the phrase *yūdō bakudan*, "guided missile.")

Another realm of planning in Japan, one that concerns us directly in this study, is similarly neither indicative nor decorative. It is the Fiscal Investment and Loan Plan (FILP) (Zaisei Tōyūshi Keikaku), called a plan both because it includes a large measure of central direction of the economy and to disguise its status as a budget. It is popularly known as the "second budget." Almost 50 percent of the size of the official national budget, its funds are used to finance the national policy companies and public corporations of Japan. From its origins in 1953 until early 1973, when Socialist party Diet member Tanaka Sumiko publicly complained about its secretive administration, the FILP was totally under the control of the economic bureaucrats and was used to promote the plans they approved.[17] Today it is submitted to the Diet along with the General Account Budget for parliamentary approval, but it is still a major fiscal planning institution of the Japanese government. I shall devote a later chapter to its origins, source of funds, size, and administration.

---

[15] Watanabe Tsunehiko, "National Planning and Economic Development: A Critical Review of the Japanese Experience," *Economics of Planning*, vol. 10, nos. 1-2 (1970), pp. 21-51.

[16] Shiroyama Saburō, "Tsūsan kanryō jinbutsu shōshi" [A short history of the bureaucratic personnel in trade and industry], *Chūō kōron*, August 1975, p. 317.

[17] For the decision by the Diet to require Diet approval of the FILP, see Yasuhara Kazuo, *Ōkurashō* [Ministry of Finance] (Tokyo: Kyōikusha, 1974), pp. 95-96.

In short, as the existence of these various institutions suggests, planning is a formal function in Japan; it is just not done by people in organizations called "planning agencies," who do other things.

Government's Economic Role

Plainly, then, the government's role in the Japanese economy is a complex and pervasive one. There are many ways to categorize the government's manifold activities, but one of the most direct is also one of the most authoritative. Odahashi Sadaju, former technical adviser to the Commerce and Industry Committee of the upper house of the Diet, analyzes seven major means of governmental "guidance" (*yūdō*) of the economy. The first is monetary and fiscal measures. These include long-term low-interest funds supplied to designated industries and enterprises by some of the institutions we shall be studying in this book (for example, the Japan Development Bank). Second is the tax system, primarily in the form of tax relief or suspension intended to promote exports, introduce industrial rationalization measures, foster technological development, and install pollution prevention equipment. Third is subsidies. Government has subsidized corporations and other enterprises since the Meiji period, notably in transportation and agriculture before the war, and in agriculture and mining after the war, but subsidies have never been as important as fiscal and tax measures.

A fourth means of governmental control is direct allocation or rationing systems, which allow the government to fix the amounts of a product that a factory may produce or forward. These were critical governmental powers during the 1940s and 1950s. Although their use has declined with the trade and capital liberalization policies of the 1960s, production allocation (*seisan wariate*) and shipping allocation (*shukka wariate*) are still employed to control excess production.

Fifth, and most important since the Meiji Restoration, is the government's extensive licensing and approval authority. Government has the right to give licenses granting permission to open a business, approving rates to be charged, approving annual investment plans, and governing many other business activities. This authority is typically used less to regulate an industry than to foster it. The laws surrounding the importing and refining of petroleum provide an extreme example: since 1962, governmental petroleum policy has had as a major objective the building of a nationally owned refining sector capable of competing with and displacing foreign oil companies.

A sixth means government uses to guide the economy is of primary concern in this book: direct governmental investment in industry

22

through special legal entities. The Japanese government spends sums that are comparatively small but actually large in terms of both the total government budget and the strategic value of the projects supported through 112 (as of 1975) of these entities. Examples are the Japan Petroleum Development Corporation (Sekiyu Kaihatsu Kōdan), a pure government corporation; the Electric Power Development Company (Dengen Kaihatsu K.K.), a mixed public-private enterprise; and the Japan Synthetic Rubber Company (Nihon Gōsei Gomu K.K.), a company set up by the government when it became apparent that private interests would not invest without governmental participation, but which the government subsequently sold off to private interests. The seventh and final means of governmental control is "administrative guidance" (*gyōsei shidō*), Japan's famous (or notorious, depending upon your point of view) cooperative action between the government and private firms in order to reconcile and achieve public and private objectives.[18]

This list of ways government intervenes in the economy is meant only to illustrate the potent and pervasive role the Japanese government plays in the national economy. The actual influence in Japan of the Ministry of International Trade and Industry, for instance, is closer to that of the Department of Defense in the United States than the Department of Commerce, and it will be better understood in terms of the former comparison. In this study I shall not attempt to deal with the full range of what the Japanese call commercial and industrial policy; that subject is reserved for a larger work on the history of MITI. The relationship between MITI and public enterprise lies in the fact that MITI controlled twenty-seven public corporations as of 1975, more than any other ministry or agency of the Japanese government. Yet even the less pervasive Ministry of Agriculture and Forestry controlled nineteen public corporations; the Ministry of Finance controlled sixteen; the Ministry of Transportation controlled fourteen; and the Ministry of Constructions controlled ten.

The topic of this book, then, is the nature and significance of the institutions of public enterprise in Japan.[19] In terms of Odahashi's typology, the activities of these corporations involve Japan's commercial and industrial policy; they relate to his first (monetary and fiscal powers) and sixth (direct governmental investment) categories of governmental control of the economy.

[18] Odahashi Sadaju, *Nihon no shōkō seisaku* [Japan's commercial and industrial policy] (Tokyo: Kyōiku Shuppan, 1971), pp. 26-31.
[19] For a survey of the Japanese political economy, see Chalmers Johnson, "The Japanese Problem," in Donald C. Hellmann, ed., *China and Japan: A New Balance of Power* (Lexington, Mass.: D. C. Heath, 1976), pp. 51-94.

23

2
The Types of
Public Policy Companies

Public policy companies are corporations in which some or all ownership shares are held by the government, and management is charged
with serving public policy ends rather than making a profit for the
shareholders. In the United States, Amtrak is such a corporation; so
are the Postal Service, the Tennessee Valley Authority, and some of
the nuclear weapons laboratories. In Japan, one form of public corporation, the national policy company (*kokusaku kaisha*), is defined
as "a company that is identical to a wholly private joint stock company
but in which there is cooperative investment by both state and private
capital and in which the objectives of the enterprise are important from
the point of view of national policy."[1]

Often governments choose the corporate form to achieve public
goals because it enables them to separate the costs of a particular activity from a general account budget. This can be a way of insuring
that the activity is self-supporting, or of isolating clearly the share of
government subsidy the activity is using. A government also may set
up a public corporation to insulate an activity from parliamentary or
bureaucratic politics, or to draw capital and technology into an area
that is too risky or unprofitable to attract private enterprise. On the
other hand, public corporations also have been known to serve as post-
retirement havens for bureaucrats, as dummies to camouflage government activities in sensitive areas, as ways for special interests to gain
indirect access to the public treasury, and as political compromises when
the interests of government and private capital clash.

The public corporation is a wonderfully flexible form of organization; and the Japanese probably have utilized, varied, and perfected it

---

[1] Endō Shōkichi, *Zaisei tōyūshi* [Fiscal investment and loan funds] (Tokyo:
Iwanami Shinsho No. 595, 1966), pp. 61-62.

25

more than any other open society. It is difficult simply to list the numbers and types of Japanese public policy companies because of definitional problems. Given the commitments of the Japanese government to nurturing and protecting Japanese-owned businesses, some of Japan's foreign competitors might be forgiven if they imagined that *all* companies in postwar Japan were public policy companies. No less a figure than Shiina Etsusaburō, former vice-minister of munitions and of commerce and industry, twice minister of MITI, and vice-president of the Liberal Democratic Party, gives some support to this view. During the 1920s and early 1930s, when he was a young bureaucrat in the Shōkō-shō (Ministry of Commerce and Industry, MITI's predecessor before 1949), he observed that the big businesses of Osaka were quite independent of the government. Officials of his ministry were more interested in keeping on the right side of the *zaikai* ("business world") than in attempting to guide it. But during and after the war that changed. "Today," notes Shiina, "all big companies, even those that say they are from Osaka, have their main offices in Tokyo, near the government. That was not true in the 1930s. Then the Osaka *zaikai* was in Osaka, and it was very powerful."[2]

The government does not, of course, help each and every company to prosper; witness the high rate of bankruptcies in Japan. But it is a matter of Japanese national policy, even national defense, to maintain healthy and growing industries. Access to the government inevitably has become an interest of every competent board of directors.

In this study, I am not concerned with governmental commercial and industrial policy regarding all businesses, but only with the government's instrumental use of various corporate enterprises to serve state purposes. Even in this respect, the range of governmental activities is considerably broader than supervising the operations of Japan's 112 official government corporations, the *tokushu hōjin* ("special legal entities"). Some other corporations have a more exclusively public character and employ more treasury funds than several of the *tokushu hōjin*.

For example, the Power Reactor and Nuclear Fuel Development Corporation, created in 1967, is a *tokushu hōjin,* a government corporation in the strict sense. It is 94.7 percent owned by the government, it was created by a specially enacted Diet law, and it is closely supervised by the Science and Technology Agency, a branch of the central government. On the other hand, the Japan Electronic Computer Company

---

[2]Shiina Etsusaburō, "Nihon sangyō no daijikkenjō: Manshū [Manchuria: the great proving ground for Japanese industry], *Bungei shunjū*, February 1976, pp. 108-9.

(JECC) (Nihon Denshi Keisanki K.K.) is not a "special legal entity," though it was created in 1961 by Hiramatsu Morihiko when he was deputy chief of the Electronics Industry Section, Heavy Industry Bureau, of MITI. It is financed primarily by the Japan Development Bank, which is a special legal entity; it is operated solely to bolster Japanese computer manufacturers by purchasing computers from them and leasing them to users, the development of the domestic computer industry being a high priority of national policy. Further, between 1961 and 1967, the JECC was headed by Murase Naokai, a former vice-minister of commerce and industry and one of the great "seniors" (*sempai*) of MITI, who was persuaded to take the job of president by the then sitting deputy chief of MITI's Heavy Industry Bureau, and later vice-minister, Kumagai Yoshifumi.[3] Thus, although the JECC is not a *tokushu hōjin,* it is an outstanding example of a national policy company (*kokusaku kaisha*) and must be included in any meaningful list of Japan's public corporations.

A Typology of Public Corporations

There are many public corporations in Japan comparable to the JECC. To distinguish the special legal entities from other forms of corporate enterprise, and to identify as well the public corporations that are not special legal entities, I have constructed a typology based on the proximity of an organization to its official governmental sponsor (a ministry or agency of the central government) and on the degree of direct control the official sponsor has over the corporation. This typology produces six categories, as follows:

    I. Direct government enterprises
    II. Special legal entities, narrowly defined
    III. Special legal entities, broadly defined
    IV. Auxiliary organs (*gaikaku dantai*), foundations, promotion associations, and so forth
    V. National policy companies, narrowly defined
    VI. National policy companies, broadly defined

---

3 On Hiramatsu, see Nihon Minsei Kenkyūkai, ed., *Kōkyū kanryō sōran* [General survey of higher bureaucrats] (Tokyo: Hyōron Shinsha, 1971), p. 161. On the operations of the JECC, see Eugene J. Kaplan, *Japan: The Government-Business Relationship* (Washington, D.C.: U. S. Government Printing Office, 1972), p. 87; and Organization for Economic Cooperation and Development, *The Industrial Policy of Japan* (Paris: OECD, 1972), p. 60. On Murase, Kumagai, and the JECC, see Murase Naokai-shi Tsuitōroku Hensan Iinkai, *Murase-san no omoide* [Recollections of Mr. Murase] (Tokyo: privately printed, 1970), pp. 133, 376, 724.

27

Although the primary concern in this study is the organizations of type II, an understanding of special legal entities must begin with a survey of the entire typology. This is because though the categories of the typology are fixed, the organizations may shift from one to another over time. Thus, for example, the Japanese National Railways belonged to type I before 1949 and to type II after 1949; the Japan External Trade Organization (JETRO) belonged to type IV before 1958 and to type II after 1958; and the Japan Synthetic Rubber Company, set up in 1957, moved slowly from type V to type VI during its first decade of existence. From the virtual nationalization of the electric power industry in the late 1930s through its denationalization under the Allied occupation of Japan and down to the present, the various electric companies have belonged to every category except type IV. The number of organizations in each category also has varied considerably over time, particularly in type II, which has ranged from 22 organizations in 1953 to 112 in 1975. (The appendix lists chronologically all special legal entities created after the war, plus those that remain from the prewar era.) The rest of this chapter will explain and illustrate each of the six types of public corporation.

Direct Government Enterprises

Type I includes those government agencies that provide the public with services and products that could be supplied by either a public or a private corporation. Japan has five direct government enterprises: the postal service, the forestry service, government printing (including currency and stamps), the mint, and a governmental monopoly of the manufacture of industrial alcohol. Before and during the war, there were eight: the five already listed, plus the national railways, the telephone and telegraph services, and a government monopoly over the production and sale of tobacco and salt. The last three were spun off into type II public corporations during the occupation.

All of this seems straightforward enough, but the public monopoly sector is actually much less neat than it seems. What the government does directly and what it does through public corporations cannot be explained simply as a matter of policy or of administrative rationality. The ways government intervenes in the economy are primarily the result of historical occurrences—that is, of decisions made in response to particular situations in the past. Those decisions and the institutional arrangements that grew out of them have persisted long after the historical conditions they were intended to resolve have disappeared. Thus, what is called "political culture" is more a matter of historical accumula-

28

tion and inertia than it is of national character, political philosophy, or any other cultural "trait."

One such historical situation that has had lasting effects on Japanese public corporations, and particularly the direct government enterprises, had to do with labor problems. Government enterprises always face problems of labor relations: when workers are paid out of the national treasury, they invariably have a different relationship with their employer from when they are working for a profit-making enterprise. They find themselves placed in the same category as state officials or the military, yet in terms of their actual jobs they seem closer to workers in the private sector. If they are employed by natural or political monopolies controlled by the state (postal services, the mint, and so on), the dilemma usually is not acute; but government employees of an enterprise that is divided between a competing public and private sector (as for example the railroads are in Japan) often find themselves in conflict with their employer.

During the Allied occupation of Japan, from 1945 to 1952, the Supreme Commander for the Allied Powers (SCAP) found himself badly whipsawed between apparently competing reforms he was attempting to introduce. On the one hand, he had enacted laws to promote a vigorous, free trade union movement. On the other hand, he was attempting to reform the civil service by introducing a modern merit system and by making the whole service less elitist than it had been under the Meiji Constitution. However, the new trade union movement developed in an extremely radical direction, with the most radical unions appearing in the direct government enterprises, particularly the railroads. A series of strikes crippled the railroads throughout 1947 and 1948, and the continuous disruption of the nation's largest single enterprise threatened yet another new Allied priority: the attempt to rehabilitate the Japanese economy.[4]

In 1948, General MacArthur tried to resolve these problems by separating three of the largest direct government enterprises from the civil service and organizing them as public corporations. Thus, following the orders of SCAP, the Japanese government between 1949 and 1952 set up the Japanese National Railways Corporation, the Japan Monopoly Corporation (for tobacco and salt), and the Nippon Telephone and Telegraph Corporation as independent *kōsha* (literally, "public company"), a form of *tokushu hōjin*. MacArthur's purpose was to distinguish the labor relations that are appropriate for the civil service proper

---

[4] On the railways and the labor movement during the occupation, see Chalmers Johnson, *Conspiracy at Matsukawa* (Berkeley and Los Angeles: University of California Press, 1972).

from the labor relations that should prevail in direct government enterprises and public corporations. All that he accomplished, however, was vastly to complicate Japan's labor problems.

The National Public Service Law of 1947 regulated the relations between all civil servants and their employer, the state. It gave state employees the right to organize but not the right to bargain collectively or to strike. When this law was enacted, workers in the direct government enterprises, particularly the railroad workers, violently opposed it, seeing it as an infringement on the right to strike which they had gained early in the occupation. On July 22, 1948, in an attempt both to mollify the direct government enterprise workers and to prohibit strikes in the public sector, General MacArthur wrote a letter to Prime Minister Ashida demanding that "steps be taken immediately to effect a comprehensive revision of the existing National Public Service Law."[5] The outcome of this letter was the passage, in 1948, of the Public Corporations and National Enterprises Labor Relations Law. This new law granted to workers in the five direct government enterprises and the three *kōsha* that were separated from the direct government enterprise sector the rights to organize and to bargain collectively, but it denied them the right to strike.

The 1948 law has always been resented by employees of the direct government enterprises and *kōsha* (note that Japanese nouns are both singular and plural), whose unions have been among the more radical in postwar Japan; and illegal strikes by workers in the direct enterprise and *kōsha* sectors were still one of the major sources of labor strife in Japan more than twenty-five years after the law was passed. The reason is that no further public corporations were added to the *kōsha* category during the occupation beyond the original three that MacArthur designated. All public corporations set up after them were put into other categories of *tokushu hōjin,* which fall under the nation's basic Trade Union Law, permitting workers to organize, to bargain collectively, and to strike.

Since the occupation, the government has attempted to move other direct government enterprises (for instance, the postal and alcohol services) into the public corporate sector for purposes other than improved labor relations (for instance, greater fiscal accountability). However, the unions of the powerful Sōhyō labor federation have blocked all such efforts unless the government would repeal the 1948 law and extend the same privileges to the workers in the direct government enterprises

---

[5] Supreme Commander for the Allied Powers, Monograph 13, "Reorganization of Civil Service," *Historical Monographs* (Washington, D.C.: National Archives, 1951), microfilm frame 532.

and *kōsha* that are enjoyed by workers in the other 109 *tokushu hōjin* and in private enterprise. The government, however, believes that the right to strike should not be given to the direct government enterprise employees or to the workers in the railroad, monopoly, and telephone companies. The government and the unions deadlocked over the issue, and it was still a major source of political controversy in the 1970s.

Thus, ironically, what is a direct government enterprise, a *kōsha*, or another form of public corporation in Japan is something that was indirectly determined by General MacArthur when he sought to bring the Communist-dominated public employees' unions under control. Table 3 summarizes the relationship between employees and labor laws in the five government enterprises as of early 1973.

The alcohol manufacturing activities of MITI illustrate still different labor relations problems in a direct government enterprise. In March 1937, to try to relieve its dependence on imported petroleum the gov-

Table 3
LABOR RELATIONS LAWS AND DIRECT GOVERNMENT ENTERPRISES

Government Enterprise	Controlling Ministry	National Public Service Law	Public Corporations and National Enterprises Labor Relations Law
		Number of Employees Covered by	
Postal Service	Ministry of Posts and Telecommunications	202	323,024
National Forestry Service	Forestry Agency, Ministry of Agriculture and Forestry	1,061	38,471
Printing Service	Printing Bureau, Ministry of Finance	16	7,350
Mint	Mint Bureau, Ministry of Finance	16	1,827
Alcohol Monopoly	Alcohol Department, Light Industry Bureau (later, Chemical Industry Bureau), MITI	4	1,123

Source: Administrative Management Agency, *Government Corporations in Japan* (Tokyo, 1973), pp. 50–53.

ernment passed a law creating an official alcohol monopoly, and it directed the Ministry of Commerce and Industry to manufacture alcohol as a gasoline substitute in facilities owned and operated by the government. As the war in China worsened, mixing alcohol with gasoline for private use became mandatory. Later the Ministry of Commerce and Industry turned over this activity to MITI, which carries on the production and sale of industrial alcohol to the present day.[6]

During and immediately after the war the alcohol service worked well, providing cheap alcohol to the chemical industry, using molasses, sugar cane, and other natural sources as raw materials. The government operated eight national factories (seven in 1973) and eight private ones that were chartered by the government in accordance with the Alcohol Monopoly Law. However, during the late 1950s doubts began to arise about whether the service should be continued. Demand for alcohol was still high, but increasing competition was coming from synthetic alcohol, which the petrochemical companies of Sumitomo, Mitsui, and Mitsubishi were beginning to manufacture. The latter two companies were using the old military refineries at Iwakuni and Yokkaichi, the sale of which to the former zaibatsu ("family-owned industrial empires") in the mid-1950s had already produced a furor in the Diet. Now the government began talking about selling its alcohol factories, and the protests became even louder.

During 1959 and 1960, Hashiguchi Takashi, then head of the Alcohol Department of MITI's Light Industry Bureau, and Mori Chikao, the bureau chief, proposed in the Diet that MITI sell off the Kobayashi factory in Miyazaki prefecture, somewhat as their Meiji predecessors had done with the government's factories in the 1880s. Their proposal met determined opposition in the Diet from the Socialist party, and trade unionists surrounded Hashiguchi's house and engaged him in a shoving incident. The problem, as in all contemplated sales or mergers of companies in Japan, was that the factory's enterprise union feared losing its privileges or even its existence if it were forced to merge with another well-established company union. The result of this fight was that MITI resigned itself to staying in the alcohol business until it could think of some way to dismiss or reemploy the 1400 to 1500 employees then involved. It has yet to come up with a solution other than slow attrition.

Having decided to continue with government-manufactured alcohol, MITI sought to acquire a capability in synthetic alcohol—an effort that affords us an excellent example of the creation of a type V national

---

[6] Charles B. Fahs, *Government in Japan: Recent Trends in Its Scope and Operations* (New York: Institute of Pacific Relations, 1940), p. 47.

policy company. In early 1960, Mizuma Mitsuji succeeded Hashiguchi as head of the Alcohol Department, and he worked under the new Light Industry Bureau chief, Kurahachi Tadashi. After investigating the possibility of producing synthetic alcohol for toilet articles, detergents, and paint, they decided to join with three smaller, private firms with considerable experience in that area to create a jointly managed, cooperatively financed company—the Japan Synthetic Alcohol Company (Nihon Gōsei Arukōru K.K.).

With government financing and a new factory at Kawasaki, the company received its first manufacturing commission on April 28, 1965—from the government—and in August went into operation. On Kurahachi's direction, Mizuma retired as a career bureaucrat and became executive director (*senmu torishimariyaku*) of the new company. No impropriety or conflict of interest was seen in this because Mizuma's last job immediately before retiring had been as head of the MITI bureau in Sendai, and it was recognized from the outset that the company would require an *amakudari* ("descended from heaven") bureaucrat to "coordinate" (*chōsei*) the public and private interests involved. The company is not a *tokushu hōjin,* but a private profit-making firm under governmental influence. MITI's purpose in setting it up was to ensure an adequate supply of synthetic alcohol and to help three smaller firms unite and compete more effectively with the zaibatsu giants.[7]

To conclude, it should be noted that direct government enterprises dominate relatively few activities in Japan—postal services, printing, mint, forestry, and alcohol. Many more public services and utilities are provided by public corporations. Like the three *kōsha,* these government enterprises are more a historical accident than the product of any rational choice.

One influence on the growth of public corporations was the so-called Dodge Line, named after the Detroit banker Joseph M. Dodge, who was serving as a SCAP financial adviser. The Dodge Line was created in 1949 to curb inflation and to force economic retrenchment on the Japanese government. One of its results was that the principle of maintaining balanced and even over-balanced budgets became firmly entrenched in the Japanese political culture. This extreme fiscal conservatism lasted from 1949 until 1966; and it had two important unintended consequences.

---

[7] See the memoirs of Mizuma Mitsuji in Sangyō Seisaku Kenkyūjo, ed., *Tsūsan-shō 20-nen gaishi* [An unofficial twenty-year history of MITI] (Tokyo: Sangyō Seisaku Kenkyūjo, 1970), pp. 101-2, 260. Also see MITI, *Tsūshō sangyō-shō nijū nenshi* [Twenty-year history of MITI] (Tokyo: MITI, 1969), pp. 240-41.

The first consequence, to be discussed in detail in chapter 4, was to generate three separate national budgets: the general account, which until 1965 the government always balanced; the special accounts, which were oriented toward named projects and were carefully segregated and audited; and the investment budget, or Fiscal Investment and Loan Plan, which was used to finance public corporations and as an instrument of fiscal policy. As we shall see, it is not true, as some writers have suggested, that Japan relied exclusively on monetary policy and eschewed fiscal policy between 1949 and 1965; this was true only of the main general account budget.

Second, and more directly relevant to the present discussion, the emphasis on balanced budgets led to the commercialization of governmental services by means of public corporations. One reason for the tremendous expansion of public corporations in Japan during the 1950s and 1960s was the government's determination to keep its accounts in balance and to put new services on a "pay their own way" basis. The public corporation, with its separate management and accounting, was found to be an excellent vehicle for accomplishing this.[8] In Japan, people pay public corporations directly for many governmental services that are provided free in other societies; at the same time, the Japanese enjoy one of the lowest tax burdens of any OECD nation. The relatively low level of direct governmental activity is merely the other side of the coin of an extremely active public corporate sector, to which we now turn.

Special Legal Entities, Narrowly Defined

Public corporations in the strictly legal sense (that is, *tokushu hōjin,* or "special legal entities") perform a myriad of functions that touch the lives of all Japanese and many foreigners. They range from the big construction enterprises (Japan Housing Corporation, Japan Highway Public Corporation, New Tokyo International Airport Corporation, and so forth) through companies involved in agriculture, social welfare, and energy development, down to the Japan Foundation, the International Cooperation Agency, and the National Space Development Agency.

In 1972, the then 113 *tokushu hōjin* spent 80 percent of the funds in the Fiscal Investment and Loan Plan, which was itself 49.1 percent of the general account budget and 6.3 percent of gross national product. During 1974, the *tokushu hōjin* employed 821 full-time executives, 260 part-time executives, and 919,743 workers. In 1973, of 384 members of the boards of directors of the 61 most influential *tokushu hōjin,*

---

[8] Yoshitake Kiyohiko, *An Introduction to Public Enterprise in Japan* (Beverly Hills, Cal.: Sage Publications, 1973), p. 112.

303 were retired officials (Japanese officials retire at age fifty-five or under) from the ministries that controlled the corporations. In a most direct sense, though not in the legal sense, these corporations are operational extensions of the central government bureaucracy, which is itself one of the most intrusive public services in any open industrial society.[9]

The definition of a *tokushu hōjin* is both extremely complex and quite vague, reflecting the comparative lack of interest in Japan in legal consistency when it comes to matters of vital national importance. In the final analysis, the definition of a Japanese public corporation is arbitrary: it is any public corporation that the Ministry of Finance agrees to pay for and that the Administrative Management Agency of the Prime Minister's Office designates as such.[10] The reasons why either of these official agencies decides to pay for or to recognize a special legal entity are matters not of law or of general policy but of political bargaining within the central government, sometimes involving pressure from the Liberal Democratic Party and occasionally from the Diet or the public.

A *tokushu hōjin* (literally, "special juridical person") is one form of corporate enterprise recognized by Japanese law. The term *tokushu hōjin* refers to corporations that have been created by separate, Diet-enacted laws, which spell out the structure, governance, functions, financing, and so forth of the corporation. Other forms of corporate enterprise include ordinary joint stock companies (*kabushiki kaisha,* abbreviated K.K.) and related entities created in accordance with the provisions of the Commercial Code; and nonprofit incorporated foundations (*zaidan hōjin*), incorporated associations (*shadan hōjin*), and related entities created in accordance with the provisions of the Civil Code. *Tokushu hōjin* may operate like, and be called, *kabushiki kaisha* or other general forms of corporation, but they are created by special laws and not under the terms of the Commercial or the Civil Code. Several types of corporate enterprise within the category *tokushu hōjin* (such as *kōsha, kōdan,* and others, discussed below) can only be special legal entities.

---

[9] See Fukushima Ryōichi (chief, General Affairs Section, Financial Bureau, Ministry of Finance), Yamaguchi Mitsuhide (chief, First Fund Planning and Operations Section, Financial Bureau, Ministry of Finance), and Ishikawa Itaru (chief, Second Fund Planning and Operations Section, Financial Bureau, Ministry of Finance), *Zaisei tōyūshi* [Fiscal investment and loan funds] (Tokyo: Ōkura Zaimu Kyōkai, 1973), pp. 66-67; Gyōsei Kanri Chō [Administrative Management Agency], *Tokushu hōjin sōran* [General survey of special legal entities] (Tokyo: Ōkura-shō Insatsu-kyoku, 1975), p. 312; and "Seiryokyo Unions Stage Pay, Protest Strikes," *Japan Times,* March 21, 1974, p. 2.

[10] Administrative Management Agency, *Government Corporations in Japan* (Tokyo, 1973), p. 49; idem, *Tokushu hōjin sōran* (1975 ed.), p. 302.

35

Another complexity relates to the fact that although all public corporations in the legal sense are *tokushu hōjin*, not all *tokushu hōjin* are public corporations. The category *tokushu hōjin* includes all juridical persons that have been created by special laws, and this takes in such things as local legal entities and many banks, schools, hospitals, and so forth. Therefore, within the category of *tokushu hōjin*, the ones that are public enterprises and national policy companies of the central government are those that the Ministry of Finance has approved and that are subject to inspection by the Administrative Management Agency. The ultimate test of a *tokushu hōjin* in this narrow sense is that it is listed in the annual *Tokushu hōjin sōran* (General Survey of Special Legal Entities), published by the Administrative Management Agency. This volume surveys only those *tokushu hōjin* subject to the agency's examination, and not the several thousand *tokushu hōjin* in the broad sense.

In short, then, a special legal entity, narrowly defined, is a corporate enterprise created by a special law and designated by the government as a public enterprise; it may take the form of an ordinary joint stock company, a foundation, or a mutual aid association, or it may take one of several special forms that are reserved for public corporations. In this study, I follow normal Japanese governmental parlance in using the term *tokushu hōjin* as a shorthand way to refer to the 112 (as of 1975) designated corporate entities, although *tokushu hōjin* actually includes a much larger group of corporations, some of which belong to our type III.

Almost all the special legal entities have been created since World War II. Their numbers over the years are difficult to calculate, as we shall see in the following chapter; but in 1940 there were about a hundred "special companies" in the Japanese Empire, different in names and forms but analogous to those existing today. Of the hundred, about thirty were located in Japan, about fifty in Manchuria, and about twenty in occupied China.[11] Only six of these survived Japan's defeat and the occupation reforms and still exist today: one created in 1923, two in 1936, and one each in 1939, 1941, and 1944. Table 4 details the increase in special legal entities since 1946. Between 1954 and 1974, an average of over four new public corporations were created every year.

The 112 government corporations of 1975 can be classified in many different ways: in terms of their basic functions (money lending, money spending, price stabilization, and so forth); in terms of their sectoral concerns (industrial development, transportation, social welfare,

---

[11] Noda Keizai Kenkyūjo, *Senjika no kokusaku kaisha* [National policy companies during wartime] (Tokyo: Noda Keizai Kenkyūjo, 1940), p. 2.

Table 4
NUMBER OF SPECIAL LEGAL ENTITIES, 1946–1974

Year	Number	Year	Number	Year	Number
1946	6	1960	65 (+4)	1968	109 (+1, −5)
1953	22	1961	71 (+6)	1969	110 (+2, −1)
1954	25 (+3)	1962	81 (+10)	1970	112 (+5, −3)
1955	33 (+8)	1963	94 (+14, −1)	1971	112 (0)
1956	39 (+6)	1964	99 (+5)	1972	113 (+4, −3)
1957	44 (+5)	1965	104 (+7, −2)	1973	112 (−1)
1958	53 (+9)	1966	108 (+4)	1974	112 (+4, −4)
1959	61 (+8)	1967	113 (+8, −3)		

Source: Administrative Management Agency, *Tokushu hōjin sōran* [General survey of special legal entities] (Tokyo: Ōkura-shō Insatsu-kyoku, 1975), pp. 316-19.

energy); in terms of the ministries that control them (a most important classification, as we shall see in chapter 5); in terms of their degrees of independence from the Diet; and in terms of their access to the bureaucratically-controlled funds of the Fiscal Investment and Loan Plan. We could also classify the 112 core corporations in terms of their capacities to absorb retired bureaucrats into lucrative "civilian" occupations; in terms of their controlling ministries' strategies for defending their own jurisdictions against the encroachments of other ministries; in terms of their controlling ministries' strategies for expanding their spheres of influence in the ever present struggle for bureaucratic survival; or in terms of how they figure in the central ministries' indirect attempts to reverse the decentralizing reforms of the occupation and expand central government control over local government by using public corporations to preempt its functions.

Before we can make use of any of these interesting taxonomic possibilities, however, we must introduce the official typology of public policy companies and its unique vocabulary. The official typology is frankly confusing—even to many Japanese officials.[12] It is well to recognize at the outset, therefore, as these lists of possible organizing principles suggest, that the official typology, important as it is, is not

---

[12] Yoshitake, *Public Enterprise in Japan*, pp. 12-13; Administrative Management Agency, *Government Corporations in Japan*, p. 14.

a strictly rational or legal way of classifying public corporations. The official typology serves at least in part to obfuscate the situation so that the outside observer will not grasp easily what is going on. Public corporations in Japan, as elsewhere, are part of the world of public administration as understood by planners, economists, and other rationalists. They are also part of the world of the bureaucrat and of his absolute requirement to maintain or expand his bureau's jurisdiction, on which his own security depends. And in addition to reason and bureaucratic interest, the following set of categories is the product of history and the complexity it generates.

During 1975, the 112 designated special legal entities were subdivided by the government into the following official types. The translations are only rough equivalents; normally the Japanese names are used without translation in discussions of Japanese public enterprises. The term *kōdan* was, in fact, introduced by SCAP during the occupation.

3 *kōsha* (public corporations)

15 *kōdan* (public units)

20 *jigyōdan* (enterprise units)

10 *kōko* (public finance corporations)

2 *tokushu ginkō* (special banks)

2 *kinko* (depositories)

1 *eidan* (wartime term for *kōdan*)

12 *tokushu kaisha* (special companies, or mixed public-private enterprises)

47 other, including 7 *kikin* (funds, or endowments), 7 *shinkōkai* (promotion associations), 5 *kenkyūkai* (research associations), and 5 *kyōsai kumiai* (mutual aid asssociations).

The three *kōsha* are the Japanese National Railways Corporation, the Japan Monopoly Corporation, and the Nippon Telephone and Telegraph Corporation. As we have already seen, these are the three former government departments that the American occupation authorities ordered separated from their former ministries and set up as independent public corporations. In 1974, the *kōsha* employed 781,438 of the total of 919,743 workers in the public corporate sector; these were also the only public corporation employees covered by the Public Corporations and National Enterprises Labor Relations Law.

The *kōsha* are the most public of all the *tokushu hōjin*. Although they maintain independent accounts, their budgets are subject to Diet approval; and contrary to the theory of the public corporation, they are under heavy political pressure, which may account for the conspicuous lack of efficiency of at least one of them, the railroads. All the fixed capital of the three *kōsha* is supplied by the government, and the railroad and telephone companies have access to loans from the Fiscal Investment and Loan Plan (FILP). The Ministry of Transportation controls the railroads; the Ministry of Posts and Telecommunications looks after the telephone company; and the Ministry of Finance runs the tobacco and salt monopoly.

Since all three *kōsha* are familiar examples of natural or political monopolies in corporate form, we shall not have anything further to say about them except to note that the Japan Monopoly Corporation is a major revenue-raising agency of the central government. Its profits (¥864,332 million in 1970) are divided between local special legal entities (our type III) and the national treasury.[13]

The fifteen *kōdan* are the heart of the public enterprise sector. They invest huge sums supplied by the FILP, primarily in large-scale public works and construction projects. Although most of the capital for the *kōdan* is supplied by the FILP or from *kōko*, some of it has come from loans from life insurance companies or the World Bank.

Kōdan are more independent than either *kōsha or kōko*. Both the latter must submit their budgets and annual business plans to a Diet vote, whereas the *kōdan* are only subject to the approval of their supervising ministers. On the other hand, *kōsha* and *kōko* exist until the laws establishing them are repealed, whereas the *kōdan* are normally based on so-called sunset laws—legislation with a fixed expiration date.

The Japan Housing Corporation, created in 1955, is a *kōdan*; it builds the innumerable *danchi* or modern apartment houses that fill the suburbs of big cities. Another *kōdan* is the Internal Passenger Ship Corporation of 1959, which constructs light wooden and steel ships for carrying passengers and mail between small domestic ports. The Keihin Port Development Authority and the Hanshin Port Development Authority, both of 1967, are *kōdan* responsible for enlarging the Tokyo and Osaka-Kobe harbors to accommodate 200,000-ton tankers and for providing container facilities. And the Industrial Relocation and Coal Production Areas Promotion Corporation of 1972 is a *kōdan,* created to

---

[13] There are voluminous sources on the *kōsha*. For example, see Taura Ken, "Nihon Denshin Denwa Kōsha" [The Nippon Telephone and Telegraph Corporation], *Kankai* [Bureaucratic World], vol. 2, no. 5 (May 1976), pp. 114-22; and Nihon Denshin Denwa Kōsha, *Denshin denwa jigyōshi* [History of the telephone and telegraph industry], 7 vols. (Tokyo: Denki Tsūshin Kyōkai, 1959).

implement former Prime Minister Tanaka's grandiose scheme for the "reform of the Japanese archipelago."[14]

An example of a foreign-funded *kōdan* is the Aichi Prefecture Water Resources Corporation (Aichi Yōsui Kōdan), created in 1955 and abolished in 1968, with Hamaguchi Takehiko, the son of the prewar prime minister, as president. This company built dams in Nagano prefecture and canals in Gifu prefecture to irrigate the Chita peninsula, south of Nagoya in Aichi prefecture. It was initially financed by yen counterpart funds from the purchase and sale of United States surplus agricultural commodities (a subject to which we shall return in chapter 4) and a $1.1 million loan from the World Bank.

The twenty *jigyōdan* are merely smaller *kōdan*. The chief difference between *kōdan* and *jigyōdan* is their financing. Whereas all the *kōdan* in 1973 were funded in part from the FILP, only eight of the *jigyōdan* were. This meant that most funds for the *jigyōdan* had to come from direct appropriations, through their controlling ministries, and that as a result they were less independent than the more financially secure *kōdan*.

An interesting example of a *jigyōdan*, one that *is* financed by the FILP, is the Ministry of Agriculture and Forestry's Hachirōgata New Community Development Corporation (Hachirōgata Shinnōson Kensetsu Jigyōdan). This company began in 1958 as a land reclamation project, one of many schemes at the time to provide more space for farming and industry in overcrowded Japan. The idea was to drain Hachirōgata Inlet in Akita prefecture, making land available for rice paddy and vegetable gardens and providing home sites for 9,000 families. From 1958 to 1965, the project was carried on under a special account in the second of the three national budgets. In 1965, the ministry was able to convert it into a *jigyōdan*, which as a corporation has the advantage of being able to

---

14 On the Industrial Relocation and Coal Production Areas Promotion Corporation, see Katō Takashi, *Shigen enerugī chō* [The Natural Resources and Energy Agency] (Tokyo: Kyōiku Sha, 1974), p. 66. Concerning Tanaka's development scheme, see Tanaka Kakuei, *Building a New Japan: A Plan for Remodeling the Japanese Archipelago* (Tokyo: Simul Press, 1973). On some of the other *kōdan,* see the useful series of articles in *Kankai,* as follows: Taura Ken, "Shin Tōkyō kokusai kūkō kōdan" [New Tokyo International Airport Corporation], vol. 1, no. 1 (November 1975), pp. 123-29; idem, "Nihon jūtaku kōdan" [Japan Housing Corporation], vol. 1, no. 2 (December 1975), pp. 123-29; idem, "Nihon tetsudō kensetsu kōdan" [Japan Railway Construction Corporation], vol. 2, no. 1 (January 1976), pp. 123-29; Shirahama Kenichirō, "Nōyōchi kaihatsu kōdan" [Agricultural Land Development Corporation], vol. 2, no. 2 (February 1976), pp. 123-29; Atsumi Hogara, "Chiiki shinkō setsubi kōdan [Regional Promotion and Facilities Corporation], vol. 2, no. 3 (March 1976), pp. 116-21; Taura Ken, "Nihon dōro kōdan" [Japan Highway Public Corporation], vol. 2, no. 4 (April 1976), pp. 128-35; and idem, "Takuchi kaihatsu kōdan" [Housing Land Development Corporation] [established September 1975], vol. 2, no. 6 (June 1976), pp. 156-63.

preempt retired Agriculture Ministry bureaucrats as executives. So long as the Hachirōgata project was a special account, the Ministry of Finance had a stranglehold over its operations. As a *jigyōdan* the Agriculture bureaucrats got it much more firmly in their own hands. Although we shall encounter several cases of public corporations being shifted from one category to another (for example, from a *tokushu kaisha* to a *kōdan*), this is one of the few times a ministry has upgraded a project from a special account into a public corporation. Other examples of *jigyōdan* include the Foreign Ministry's International Cooperation Agency; the Japan Nuclear Ship Development Agency, creator of the ill-fated ship *Mutsu*; MITI's Small Business Promotion Corporation; and the Postal Ministry's Post Office Life Insurance and Annuities Welfare Corporation.

The ten *kōko* are the operating arms of the central bureaucracy in the realm of public finance. All of their capital is supplied by the government, and they make loans and investments on the basis of so-called policy interest rates—that is, they do not normally make a profit but are intended to help finance risky ventures or to aid clients who do not have access to other sources of credit. *Kōko* thus play a supplementary role to the general banking system. Both their budgets and their annual plans must be approved by the Diet. They are less autonomous than Japan's two special banks (*tokushu ginkō*), even though the latter operate under the same legal restrictions and apply the same policy interest rates. The difference lies in the fact that the banks have insisted on and won greater independence in their internal management; the *kōko* are closely supervised by their responsible ministries.

A typical *kōko* is the Housing Loan Corporation (Jūtaku Kin'yū Kōko), created in 1950 and controlled jointly by the Ministries of Construction and Finance. During the 1950s it made loans to individuals and organizations of up to 75 percent of the amount of their construction costs, at 5.5 percent per annum interest, redeemable in eighteen years in the case of a wooden house and in thirty-five years for a fireproof structure. Many other *kōko* operate under MITI's "coordination and guidance" in the medium and smaller enterprises area, the lower segment of Japan's famous "dual economic structure." [15] The Smaller Business Finance Corporation (Chūshō Kigyō Kin'yū Kōko), for example, makes loans only to firms capitalized at less than ¥10 million. During the 1950s, before the complete rehabilitation of the banking system, the *kōko* played a critical role in the economy; as late as 1958

---

[15] For a survey of over a dozen public corporations in the small business sector, see Tomioka Takao, *Chūshō kigyō chō* [The Medium and Small Enterprises Agency] (Tokyo: Kyōiku Sha, 1974), pp. 63-78.

41

the funds available to them in the FILP were nearly three times the usable sums held by the Mitsubishi or the Fuji Bank.[16] Even today the *kōko* continue to guide the economy by making indicative loans. The most recently established *kōko* is the Okinawa Development Finance Corporation of 1972, controlled by the Ministry of Finance and the Okinawa Development Agency.

The two special banks (*tokushu ginkō*) are the Japan Export-Import Bank, created in 1950, and the Japan Development Bank, created in 1951. The latter is the largest of all the public finance corporations in Japan, and it has played a crucial role in Japan's postwar economic growth. Although both banks are formally controlled by the Ministry of Finance, MITI has a very strong policy influence on both of them, particularly the Kaigin (Development Bank). If the funds that are available to MITI through the Development Bank were added to the ministry's own small share of the general account budget, MITI would be revealed to wield much larger financial powers than it normally appears to. We shall return to the origins and development of the Kaigin in chapter 4, since it is one of the key organs in the Japanese government-business nexus.

Loans from either the Export-Import Bank or the Development Bank are the chief links that tie the private national policy companies (our types V and VI) to the government. Some of these links are forged through old-boy networks. For example, Matsuda Tarō, who worked as an official in the Ministry of Commerce and Industry (MCI) from 1928 to 1949 and retired as the MCI's last vice-minister before it became MITI, subsequently served as a director of the Development Bank (1952–1957). In 1957, he became executive director of the Japan Synthetic Rubber Company, created that year at the old Naval Fuel Depot at Yokkaichi; half the total capital of ¥3 billion for the company was supplied by the Development Bank.

Similarly, Kobayashi Ataru, president of the Development Bank from 1951 to 1957, backed Yamashita Tarō, the former housing king of Manchuria during the 1930s, in Yamashita's negotiations in 1957 with his old Manchurian friend (and former minister of commerce and industry), Prime Minister Kishi, to obtain Kaigin financing for the new Arabian Oil Company of Japan. It drills in the neutral zone between Kuwait and Saudi Arabia. Kobayashi later became president of Arabian Oil, as well as chairman of the Finance Ministry's Financial System Deliberation Council (Zaisei Seidō Shingikai), and he held many other top posts in the *zaikai*.

---

16 Matsumura Yutaka, *Japan's Economic Growth 1945-60* (Tokyo: Tokyo News Service, 1961), pp. 511-13.

Another example of personal and bank ties between the government and the national policy companies is the case of the Export-Import Bank and the Alaska Pulp Company. After the war Japan found itself critically short of wood pulp for paper and chemical fibers: its forests had been ravaged for wartime needs and, as a result of the defeat, it lost South Sakhalin, which had supplied nearly 50 percent of the timber for Japan's pulp production before 1945. In 1952, Sasayama Tadao, a wartime director of the privately owned but government-guaranteed Industrial Bank of Japan (a forerunner of the Kaigin) and chairman of the Holding Company Liquidation Commission during the occupation, created the Alaska Pulp Company. He began to negotiate with the American and Japanese governments for rights and financing for logging, pulp production, and loading pulp onto ships near Sitka, Alaska. Initial expenses were estimated at about $55.5 million, with 66 percent to be supplied by Japan and 34 percent by American corporations and insurance companies. After protracted negotiations, a consortium of fourteen private and three *tokushu hōjin* banks in Japan raised the Japanese share, of which the Export-Import Bank contributed 67 percent. The company went into operation in 1960.

It should be stressed that none of these relationships between the government and prominent industrialists is considered improper in Japan. The Japanese draw the distinction between the public and private realms much less rigidly than is done in the United States.

The two *kinko* are survivals from the prewar period. The Agriculture Ministry's Central Cooperative Bank for Agriculture and Forestry (Nōrin Chūō Kinko) dates from 1923 and makes loans to the numerous politically powerful agricultural cooperatives. Today all the initial government investment has been repaid, and this *kinko* does not have access to FILP funds. MITI's Bank for Commerce and Industrial Cooperatives (Shōkō Kumiai Chūō Kinko) dates from 1936 and makes loans to small businesses. Some 62.5 percent of its capital is held by the government, and it does accept loans from the FILP.

The Shōkō Chūkin, as the Bank for Commerce and Industrial Cooperatives is popularly known in its Japanese acronym, has been firmly under MITI "old-boy" control throughout most of its postwar life. From January 1947 to February 1953, the chairman of the board of this *kinko* was Toyoda Masataka, an MCI bureaucrat from 1925 to 1946, and vice-minister from October 1945 to June 1946. During his years at the bank, Toyoda built a political constituency among small businessmen; in 1953 he was elected to the House of Councillors, where he served until 1968. He became known as one of the most influential political representatives of medium and small business interests. Mean-

43

while, at the Shōkō Chūkin, Toyoda was succeeded by Murase Naokai, who served as chairman of the board from February 1953 to February 1958. Murase had been a famous prewar vice-minister of commerce and industry (December 1936 to October 1939) and director of the Bureau of Legislation intermittently from the second Konoe cabinet of 1940 through the postwar Higashikuni cabinet of 1945. After the occupation authorities purged him, Murase became a director of the Shōkō Chūkin, advancing to the chairmanship in 1953. In 1961, as noted earlier in this chapter, Murase was asked by MITI to head the new Japan Electronic Computer Company, which he did until 1967.

Murase's successor as chairman of the board of the Shōkō Chūkin was Kitano Shigeo (February 1958 to November 1967), former Mining Bureau chief at the MCI and governor of Gunma prefecture. His replacement in turn was Takagi Hajime, who was chairman of the board from November 1967 into the 1970s, after having served from 1932 to 1952 in the military's Resources Bureau, the MCI, and MITI. He retired as head of MITI's Tokyo Bureau in 1952 and went to work first as managing director (*jōmu*), then as executive director (*senmu*), of the Japan Chamber of Commerce and Industry until taking over at the bank.[17] This pattern of leadership of a *tokushu hōjin* by retired high officials from the *hōjin*'s controlling ministry is the norm, not the exception.

The sole remaining example of the once numerous wartime *eidan* is the Teito Rapid Transit Authority, that is, the Tokyo subway system, founded in 1941. Today the subway company has fully repaid the direct investment government made in it, although it still negotiates annual loans from the FILP. It is jointly controlled by the Ministries of Transport and Construction. Since the subway company is a familiar example of a utility organized as a public corporation, an arrangement found in all advanced societies, we shall delay further discussion of *eidan*—which were one of the models for the postwar *kōdan*, unwittingly sponsored by SCAP—until the next chapter on the origins of the *tokushu hōjin*.

The twelve special companies (*tokushu kaisha*) are all mixed public-private enterprises and are organized as joint stock companies (*kabushiki kaisha*). They are sometimes referred to as "national policy companies" (*kokusaku kaisha*), in the prewar sense of the term; but in this book we distinguish them from the national policy companies, such as the Japan Synthetic Rubber Company, the Japan Synthetic Alcohol Company, or the Japan Electronic Computer Company (our

17 Shōkō Kumiai Chūō Kinko, *Shōkō kumiai chūō kinko sanjūnen shi* [Thirty-year history of the Bank for Commerce and Industrial Cooperatives] (Tokyo: Shōkō Kumiai Chūō Kinko, 1969), pp. 286, 678.

type V). The *tokushu kaisha* include Japan Air Lines, about 45 percent government owned; the Okinawa Electric Power Company, created in 1973 and 99.9 percent government owned (an interesting example of the government's returning to direct involvement in the electric power business, as it was during the militarist era); and the Tōhoku (Northeast) District Development Company, 95.6 percent government owned, which originated in 1936.

The mixed enterprise form the *tokushu kaisha* exemplify became quite popular in Japan during the 1960s. It was called the "third sector" (*daisan sekutoru*) because it was alleged to be more efficient than either the purely public or the private sector. However, many authorities feel the potentialities of the form have been retarded by excessive governmental interference. Although not subject to Diet control, mixed enterprises still require the approval of their supervising ministers to issue new stock, undertake long-term borrowing, dispose of profits, or decide on programs.

At least two of the *tokushu kaisha* are more like extensions of the official bureaucracy than joint stock companies—that is, they fit the pattern of most of the other *tokushu hōjin*. One is the Japan Ammonium Sulfate Export Company, created in 1954 and controlled by MITI, though it has no governmental ownership. The company's main purpose is to control prices. Prior to 1954, MITI was plagued with complaints that the chemical fertilizer industry was exporting ammonium sulfate at prices considerably below those it was charging domestic farmers. To bring this politically sensitive issue under control, and also to stabilize prices at a level that would keep the manufacturers in business, MITI passed two laws which, among other things, established the Japan Ammonium Sulfate Export Company. The company buys up all the ammonium sulfate produced in the country, sells what is needed domestically at fixed prices, and exports the rest. If the company shows either a profit or a loss, it is shared equitably among the manufacturers. MITI's basic purpose in setting up the company was to stabilize prices; but its longer-term intention was to force rationalization on the industry and end cutthroat competition.[18]

The second *tokushu kaisha* that functions almost as an extension of government is the famous Nippon Aeroplane Manufacturing Company, created in 1959 and also controlled by MITI. The circumstances that led to the formation of this firm were long and complex, consisting mainly of long-standing bureaucratic warfare over conflicts of jurisdiction.

[18] *Tsūsan-shō 20-nen gaishi*, pp. 100, 105-6, 246; Nihon Bōeki Kenkyūkai, *Sengo Nihon no bōeki 20-nen shi* [Twenty-year history of postwar Japanese trade] (Tokyo: Tsūshō Sangyō Chōsakai, 1967), pp. 120-22; Matsumura, *Japan's Economic Growth*, p. 176.

45

Until 1943, when Prime Minister Tōjō created the Ministry of Munitions (which was a union between the MCI and the Cabinet Planning Board and therefore in MITI's bureaucratic lineage), aircraft manufacturing had been under the jurisdiction of the Ministry of Communications (Teishin-shō). After the war the Munitions Ministry was replaced by the MCI and MITI, which claimed rights of succession to the aviation industry; but the Ministry of Transportation contested their claim. The issue was moot until the end of the occupation, since MacArthur had prohibited the Japanese from having anything to do with airplanes. When the occupation ended, restoring sovereignty to Japan, the bureaucratic war broke out in full force.

In 1952 Tamaki Keizō became vice-minister of MITI (today he is president of the Tōshiba Electric Company); MITI was interested in trying to revive Japan's once flourishing aircraft manufacturing industry. Tamaki resolved the conflict by seeming to compromise: he gave jurisdiction over construction of airplanes to MITI and over navigation to Transportation. This victory is always cited in MITI histories as one of the great achievements of Tamaki's official career.

However, MITI then had to figure out how to put its newly reclaimed authority to work. Between 1954 and 1957, the ministry proposed creating a Defense Industries Equipment Corporation (Bōei Sangyō Setsubi Jigyōdan), which it hoped to finance with loans from the United States Mutual Security Administration. When the Americans indicated that they though the Japanese ought to fund their own aviation industry, and the Ministry of Finance refused to back the new *jigyōdan,* the project collapsed. Finally, one of the veterans of MITI's Heavy Industry Bureau, Akazawa Shōichi, hit upon the idea of creating a new company in cooperation with private industry. (Akazawa was with MITI from 1941 to 1971; he was chief of the Heavy Industry Bureau when he retired and today is an adviser to Fujitsū Computers, K.K., a type VI national policy company under MITI's guidance.) The company he started was the Nippon Aeroplane Manufacturing Company.

Between 1960 and 1964, the company designed, manufactured, and sold the YS-11 twin-engine transport. The company sold 46 airplanes domestically and 41 to the Philippines, Brazil, the United States (Piedmont Airlines), Canada, Argentina, and Korea. In 1970, a young section chief in the Heavy Industry Bureau remarked, "In 1964 the dream of 'a Japanese airplane in the skies of Japan' and 'a Japanese airplane in the skies of the world' was finally realized."[19] By 1975, the

---

[19] *Tsūsan-shō 20-nen gaishi,* p. 159.

46

company that Akazawa had created, now 53.8 percent government owned, was developing an engine for a proposed successor to the YS–11. The airplane business had not turned out to be as profitable as Tamaki had hoped twenty years earlier—although the company had planned to build 180 YS–11 airplanes, its orders had only reached 87. Still, MITI had shown the country and the world that Japan could build an airplane and sell it to the Americans—which was a large part of what this "special company" was all about.[20]

The final class of *tokushu hōjin* consists of the forty-seven entities simply listed as "other." These include the Ministry of Foreign Affairs' Japan Foundation (Kokusai Kōryū Kikin), an example of a *kikin* or endowment; MITI's Japan External Trade Organization (Nihon Bōeki Shinkōkai), an example of a *shinkōkai* or promotion association; MITI's Institute of the Developing Economies (Ajia Keizai Kenkyūjo), an example of a *kenkyūjo* or research association; and the Ministry of Labor's Sake Brewers Retirement Allowance Mutual Aid Association (Seishu Seizōgyō Taishoku Kyōsai Kumiai), an example of a *kyōsai kumiai* or mutual aid association. They also include the Japan Scholarship Foundation, to which the emperor contributes 50 percent of the capital; the Japan Broadcasting Corporation, controlled by the Postal Ministry; the Ministry of Education's Japan School Lunch Society; MITI's Japan Keirin (bicycle racing) Association (in the early 1950s MITI was put in charge of bicycle racing in order to clean it up and end corruption; MITI uses the association to promote the bicycle manufacturing industry and to collect fees from racing tournaments which it turns over to local public utilities); and the Northern Territories Policy Association, controlled by the Prime Minister's Office, set up to aid refugees from the Russian-occupied islands off the coast of Hokkaido that Japan believes were illegally seized at the end of World War II. These organizations are government's response to a diversity of problems and opportunities it has faced over the past thirty years, problems it has chosen to manage through the device of the public corporation.

As noted at the beginning of this discussion, the 112 companies designated as special legal entities constitute the explicit public corpo-

---

[20] For Tamaki's own account, see MITI, *Shōkō-shō sanjūgonen shōshi* [A brief thirty-five year history of the Ministry of Commerce and Industry] (Tokyo: Tsūshō Sangyō Chōsakai, 1960), p. 117; and Seisaku Jihō Sha, *Kaikoroku sengo tsūsan seisaku shi* [Recollections of postwar trade and industrial policy] (Tokyo: Seisaku Jihō Sha), 1973, p. 15. On the Defense Industries Equipment Corporation, see Akimi Jirō, *Tsūsan kanryō* [Trade and industry bureaucrats] (Tokyo: San'ichi Shobō, 1956), pp. 118-19. For Akazawa's own views, see *Tsūsan-shō 20-nen gaishi*, pp. 120-21. On Akazawa, see Seisaku Jihō Sha, *Tsūsan-shō, sono hito to soshiki* (MITI: its men and organization) (Tokyo: Seisaku Jihō Sha, 1968), pp. 403-4.

rate sector in Japan. But certain other corporations also have important implicit public policy functions. To appreciate the extent of "semi-private" governmental activity in Japan, it is necessary to examine these undesignated units as well. We therefore return to our overall sixfold typology of Japan's public policy companies.

Special Legal Entities, Broadly Defined

In 1967, the higher civil officials of the First and Second Fund Planning and Operations Sections, Financial Bureau, Ministry of Finance, had available for distribution in the FILP some ¥2,388,400,000,000 (approximately $6.6 billion at the prevailing exchange rate of US$1 = ¥360). In 1973, the total was ¥6,924,800,000,000 (approximately $23.8 billion at the prevailing exchange rate of US$1 = ¥300). They planned to allocate these funds according to the following general scheme (percentages are approximate):

(1) Special accounts	1 percent
(2) *Kōsha*	10 percent
(3) *Kōko, tokushu ginkō*, etc.	44 percent
(4) *Kōdan, jigyōdan*, etc.	25 percent
(5) Local public entities	19 percent
(6) *Tokushu kaisha*	1 percent

Thus categories 2, 3, 4, and 6—that is, the designated *tokushu hōjin*— were scheduled to receive 80 percent of the FILP (in 1967 this amounted to ¥1,907,800,000,000). The remainder went to the special accounts (for example, the National Hospitals Special Account) and to the group of immediate concern here—our type III public policy companies, or the "local public entities" (*chihō kōkyō dantai*).

At the end of March 1973, there were 3,324 of these local public entities. When they are added to special districts and local development corporations (such as the Mutsu Ogawara Development Company in Aomori prefecture, established in 1971), the total rises to 6,246. They include prefectural, city, town, and village governments, plus locally established public entities for transportation, port, and tourist facilities. Their sole interest to us in this book is that collectively they receive each year slightly under 20 percent of the FILP (18.2 percent in 1973).

The local public entities are one form of *tokushu hōjin*. Since the end of the occupation they have been slowly declining in importance, as their functions have been preempted by the national *tokushu hōjin*. However, during the 1970s various movements for local control may have reinvigorated them, although this has not been reflected in FILP

48

allocations. They are not disaggregated in the FILP, and they are mentioned here only because they constitute a distinct type of Japanese public policy company.[21]

Auxiliary Organs, Foundations, Promotion Associations, and Others

All the organizations in this category, type IV in our typology, are formally private. They usually take the form of incorporated foundations (*zaidan hōjin*), incorporated associations (*shadan hōjin*), or "unions" (*kumiai*) of one kind or another, as authorized under the Civil Code. They are all either nonprofit or noncommercial enterprises. Leon Hollerman signals their importance when he observes that the government and the business community have two main conduits for communications. One is through retired government officials reemployed as executives in private, profit-making enterprises—so-called *amakudari* ("descent from heaven"). The other is via "institutes, trade associations, and research groups of one kind or another, which have a quasi-official status, are staffed chiefly by former government officials and are supported partly by government and partly by [Liberal Democratic] party funds." [22]

According to an investigation made by the Administrative Management Agency, in 1971 there were 4,396 of these organizations, collectively known as *gaikaku dantai* (auxiliary organs).[23] Among the organizations listed by MITI as *gaikaku dantai,* the following are chosen at random as illustrations: the Japan Banana Importers Association, the Asian Packaging Federation, the Institute of Energy Economics, the Japan General Merchandise Promotion Center, the Japan Productivity Center, the Patent Attorneys' Association of Japan, and the Japan Towel Inspection Foundation.[24]

---

[21] Fukushima et al., *Zaisei tōyūshi,* pp. 253, 585; Katō Hiroshi, ed., *Nihon no kōkigyō* [Japan's Public Enterprises] (Tokyo: Nihon Keizai Shimbunsha, 1968), pp. 256, 262; and Yoshitake, *Public Enterprise in Japan,* p. 295.

[22] Leon Hollerman, *Japan's Dependency on the World Economy* (Princeton: Princeton University Press, 1967), pp. 158-59.

[23] See Ino Kenji and Hokuto Man, *Amakudari kanryō* [Descended-from-heaven bureaucrats] (Tokyo: Nisshin Hōdō, 1972), pp. 151-53. The Ministry of Education had the largest number (1,377). The *Tsūsan handobukku* [MITI Handbook] for 1970 lists some 560 *gaikaku dantai* attached to MITI. Other ministries support equally large numbers. See Tsūsan Handobukku Henshū Iinkai, *Tsūsan handobukku* (Tokyo: Shōkō Kaikan, 1970), pp. 6, 329-590. Also see Nawa Tarō, *Tsūsan-shō* [MITI] (Tokyo: Kyōiku Sha, 1974), p. 155.

[24] MITI Information Office, *MITI Handbook* (Tokyo: Japan Trade and Industry Publicity, Inc., 1975), pp. 179-258.

Ōta Kaoru, the former chairman of the Sōhyō labor federation (1958–1966) and a severe critic of the bureaucracy, believes that the *gaikaku dantai* often serve as hiding places for slush funds, which business and public corporation executives provide for high-ranking government bureaucrats to use for overseas junkets, entertaining, golf club fees, and so forth.[25] Whatever overt and covert functions the *gaikaku dantai* may perform for the various ministries and agencies with which they are affiliated, they are relevant to this study of public policy companies for five reasons. First, when a ministry fails to convince the Ministry of Finance that it should be allowed to create a new *tokushu hōjin*, it may set up the proposed unit anyway—but as a private *gaikaku dantai*. Second, several of the most important designated *tokushu hōjin* began as *gaikaku dantai* and were later converted to special legal entities by their supporting ministries when the financial and bureaucratic conditions were propitious. Third, many active government officials, not just retired ones, serve for short terms in the *gaikaku dantai*. Fourth, some of the most important public entities in Japan, indistinguishable in form and function from *tokushu hōjin*, exist as *gaikaku dantai*, usually for political reasons. Fifth, regular agencies of the central government, wholly staffed by active duty officials, may be disguised as private foundations or associations for reasons of national policy. Many (but certainly not all) *gaikaku dantai* are thus public corporations in everything but name.

An example of a *gaikaku dantai* set up in lieu of a *tokushu hōjin* is the Information Technology Promotion Agency (Jōhō Shori Shinkō Jigyō Kyōkai), created by MITI in 1970. Based on reports of the ministry's main advisory council in 1969, MITI officials concluded that they needed a new *tokushu hōjin* in the computer software field. They wanted to use it to develop new programs and software for the domestically produced computer hardware that the Japan Electronic Computer Company was purchasing from manufacturers and leasing to clients. MITI knew that it would be difficult to get the proposed *jigyōdan* past the Budget Bureau of the Ministry of Finance; Iizuka Shirō, then chief of the Accounts Section of the MITI Secretariat, recorded his apprehension in taking the fiscal 1970 budget to the Ministry of Finance because it had a new, expensive *tokushu hōjin* in it.[26] As it turned out, Iizuka's fears were justified. For budgetary reasons the Finance Ministry authorized the proposed software *jigyōdan* only as a *kyōkai* (association). MITI was not happy, but it managed to achieve most of what it wanted

25 Ōta Kaoru, *Yakunin o kiru* [Cutting down the bureaucrats] (Tokyo: Tōyō Keizai Shinpōsha, 1973), pp. 249-50.
26 *Kōkyū kanryō sōran* (1970 ed.), p. 166.

anyway. The ministry promptly retired Kawada Michiyoshi, then head of the International Economic Department of the International Trade Bureau, and sent him off to the *kyōkai* as its civilian executive director. To serve as chairman of the board, MITI chose the prestigious Kitano Shigeo; as noted in the previous discussion of *tokushu hōjin*, he had just resigned in 1967 as chairman of the board of the Bank for Commerce and Industrial Cooperatives. The Information Technology Promotion Agency was and is today actually a *jigyōdan* in everything but name, status, and funding.[27]

A prime example of a special legal entity that began as an auxiliary organ is the Japan External Trade Organization, originally known as the Japan External Trade Recovery Organization (JETRO). Ueno Kōshichi, vice-minister of MITI from June 1957 to May 1960 (and after that executive director of the Kansai Electric Power Company), recalls that JETRO's predecessor, the Overseas Trade Promotion Association (Kaigai Bōeki Shinkōkai), was incorporated as a *zaidan hōjin* in 1951. Backed by the Osaka government and the Osaka *zaikai,* the organization was set up to try to expand exports and thereby contribute to economic recovery. By 1958, however, MITI had come to regard it as far too conservative and wanted to take it over and turn it into what one English commentator has called a "world-wide [commercial] intelligence service." [28] Ueno did not have an easy time creating the modern JETRO. After bitter conflicts with the Foreign Ministry, which saw the proposed agency as a clear infringement of its jurisdiction, MITI finally succeeded in persuading the Diet to pass the Japan Trade Promotion Association Law (Nihon Bōeki Shinkōkai Hō, 1958), which set up JETRO as a *tokushu hōjin* of the class "other" under MITI's supervision.

All of JETRO's funds are supplied by the government. It operates in forty-nine countries, where it has set up eighteen large Japan Trade Centers in key cities as well as forty additional offices. JETRO has approximately 180 officers in overseas service, of whom about 50 are active-duty MITI bureaucrats. Their functions are to investigate foreign markets, to publicize new Japanese products, to participate in international trade expositions, and to serve domestic and foreign business-

---

[27] On Kawada and Kitano, see Seisaku Jihō Sha, *Nihon no kanchō* [Japanese government agencies] (Tokyo: Seisaku Jihō Sha, 1974), s.v. "MITI," pp. 67, 157; and *Jinji kōshinroku* [Who's Who in Japan], 1975 ed., s.v. "Kitano Shigeo." For a short biography of Kawada, see *Tsūsan-shō, sono hito to soshiki,* pp. 134-35. On MITI's basic planning for the *jigyōdan,* see *Tsūsan-shō 20-nen gaishi,* p. 211.

[28] P. B. Stone, *Japan Surges Ahead: The Story of an Economic Miracle* (New York: Praeger, 1969), p. 49.

men. Although legally a public corporation, JETRO is actually a detached bureau of MITI.[29]

Ministerial officials are regularly lent to one or another of the *gaikaku dantai* when it serves the interests of their ministries to do so. This does not mean that the recipient organization has become a public corporation under the control of the ministry, but it is further evidence of the close cooperation the government maintains with ostensibly private trade organizations. For example, Sekiyama Yoshihiko, chief in 1968 of the Technical Cooperation Section of MITI's Trade Promotion Bureau, spent three years in Cairo during the mid-sixties as head of the local office of the Japan Plant Association, a *shadan hōjin* organized to facilitate the export of complete factories. He was a good choice for what was essentially a technical aid mission, since he was an engineering graduate and a specialist in electricity.[30] During 1975, at least 196 active duty MITI officials were serving in various special legal entities, and 52 more were in *gaikaku dantai*.[31]

One major organization that has stayed a *gaikaku dantai* largely for political reasons is the well-known Japan Productivity Center (Nihon Seisansei Honbu), created in 1955 at the urging of the United States. It is and has been from the beginning a foundation (*zaidan hōjin*). The purpose of the center was to bring Japanese businessmen and executives to the United States so they could become familiar with advanced technology and production methods. During its first three years, the center sent over seventy-seven inspection teams to the United States and Europe, teams that included about 820 business and labor leaders.

Under the terms of a memorandum signed April 7, 1955, by the minister of foreign affairs and the United States ambassador, the United States agreed to pay the expenses of the inspection teams in the United States and to provide some $206,000 during 1955 to support the center in Japan. This subsidy rose to $1,200,000 for 1958. The Americans' purpose in aiding the center was to contribute to economic growth by raising productivity; this plan was based on similar projects that had been undertaken in Europe under the Marshall Plan. The center was always popular with the *zaikai* in Japan, but the Sōhyō labor federation, the Socialist party, and the Communist party denounced it as a form of "U.S. imperialism" and an attempt to break up trade unions by automating factories. All authorities agree that the center contributed sub-

---

[29] For Ueno's recollection, see *Tsūsan jyānaru*, May 24, 1975, pp. 32-33; and *Kaikoroku sengo tsūsan seisaku shi*, p. 74. On JETRO, see Odahashi Sadaju, *Nihon no shōkō seisaku* [Japan's commercial and industrial policy] (Tokyo: Kyōiku Shuppan, 1971), p. 78.

[30] *Tsūsan-shō, sono hito to soshiki*, pp. 156-57.

[31] *Tsūsan handobukku* (1976 ed.), pp. 353-59.

52

stantially to Japan's phenomenal growth in productivity (and continues to do so long after the American assistance has ended); but the ministries have been just as happy to leave it in *zaikai* hands, even though the Japanese government supplies funds to it, because of its politically controversial character.[32]

Last in the "other" category are the dummy companies set up to carry on trade with either mainland China or Taiwan. As early as 1955, MITI established a private Japan-China Export-Import Union (Nitchū Yushutsunyū Kumiai) to carry on low-level trade with the mainland. The union was not intended to, and did not, deceive any Chinese or Japanese; its purpose was to deflect pressure from the United States, which was then insisting that Japan enforce rigorously the Battle Act and the embargo against Communist China. Although the union was managed by MITI's International Trade Bureau, the government could disclaim responsibility for its activities by saying that it was a private organization.[33]

Exactly the reverse situation prevailed by 1977. The bronze plaque on what was the de facto Japanese Embassy in Taiwan now reads "Taipei Representative Office, Interchange Association, a Non-profit Foundation." The Interchange Association (Kōryū Kyōkai) had as its local chief Urabe Toshio, former Japanese ambassador to the Philippines; Urabe headed a group of Japanese officials "on loan" from the Foreign and other ministries (two of them were MITI men) as large as the staff at the United States Embassy. So far, Chinese on both sides of the Taiwan straits have found tolerable, even welcome, this display of Japanese versatility in the use of a semigovernmental organization to resolve a difficult situation.[34]

National Policy Companies, Narrowly Defined

Before the war, the term "national policy company" was used primarily to refer to what today are the "special companies" (*tokushu kaisha*) of our type II, the special legal entities. They were joint stock companies established by special laws. Among them were the South Manchurian Railroad Company (established in 1906), the Yalu River Extraction and Lumber Company (1908), the Japan Steel Company (1934), the Imperial Oil Company (1941), and the Imperial Mining Development Company (1939). Government and private interests

---

[32] Tsūshō Sangyō-shō, *Sangyō gōrika hakusho* [Industrial rationalization white paper] (Tokyo: Nikkan Kōgyō Shimbunsha, 1957), p. 18.
[33] Akimi, *Tsūsan kanryō*, p. 39.
[34] *Wall Street Journal*, March 25, 1977.

shared both their ownership and their management; in addition, the Imperial Household was a frequent investor in these companies. Their exact equivalents, without, of course, the imperial investments, are the postwar *tokushu kaisha,* the first of which was the Electric Power Development Company, founded in 1952, followed by Japan Air Lines in 1953, the Petroleum Resources Development Company in 1955, and the Nippon Aeroplane Manufacturing Company in 1959. The press still sometimes refers to the postwar *tokushu kaisha* as "national policy companies" (*kokusaku kaisha*), though this is not a technical or a legal term for them and thus is a source of considerable confusion.

Even before the war, there were a few companies not based on special laws that analysts called "quasi national policy companies."[35] Prior to the Manchurian Incident there were five of them: the two Meiji-era merchant shipping companies, Osaka Shōsen (founded in 1884) and the N.Y.K. Line (1885); the Japan-Russia Fishing Company (1914); and North Sakhalin Petroleum and North Sakhalin Mining, both started in 1926. Their "quasi" status derived solely from the fact that they were not based on special laws; their origins lay in governmental initiatives, often the result of international treaties, the sale of direct government enterprises, or governmental projects in which private firms invested only because the government asked them to and because it guaranteed both their equity and their profits. It is this type of private firm I call national policy companies strictly defined, and that are generally described in Japan today by that phrase.

Although the distinction cannot be made rigorously, I separate these firms from national policy companies broadly defined (our type VI), by the fact that the latter are not normally (or are only extremely indirectly) financed by the government. The initiative for their creation is more in *zaikai* than governmental hands. Postwar national policy companies of both kinds can be distinguished from general private enterprises in that they have what Japanese writers call a *miuchi ishiki* ("consciousness of kinship") with the government.[36] General private enterprises in industries such as textiles or electronics may be subject to strong governmental guidance or regulation, but they do not have the national policy companies' consciousness of kinship, which is usually based on the circumstances of their creation. Since the definitions in this area are more subtle than among our types I to IV, there is no possibility of making an exact count of the type V and VI national policy companies.

---

[35] Noda Keizai Kenkyūjo, *Senjika no kokusaku kaisha,* p. 4.
[36] See, for example, Nawa, *Tsūsan-shō,* p. 42.

Narrowly defined national policy companies are sometimes described by the metaphor of *sokusei saibai* ("raising out-of-season crops using artificial heat"). They are located in sectors that the government wants to see developed but that are too risky or unprofitable to attract private capital. The Japan Electronic Computer Company, discussed near the start of this chapter, belongs to this category. Another good example is the Japan Synthetic Rubber Company of 1957. Efforts to produce synthetic rubber began in Germany during World War I; the large-scale manufacture of synthetic rubber started during World War II in the United States. By 1956, synthetic rubber amounted to 42 percent of the world's total output of rubber. During the mid-1950s, in order to cut Japan's imports of both natural and synthetic rubber, MITI began discussing with firms such as Mitsubishi Petrochemical, Sanyō Chemical, Furukawa Chemical, Yokohama Rubber, and Bridgestone Tire the possibility of developing a domestic synthetic rubber industry. Given the risks involved, the companies and the government decided that the new industry should be a national policy company, with half the capital supplied by the Development Bank and the other half by the private corporations. However, the private enterprises also insisted that MITI agree that in the future, as the demand and the profitability increased, purely private synthetic rubber companies could be set up. MITI accepted this condition, and caused the Diet to enact the Law Concerning Special Measures for the Japan Synthetic Rubber Company in 1957, which made the company technically a *tokushu hōjin* but not one so designated by the Administrative Management Agency. Matsuda Tarō, former MITI vice-minister and former director of the Development Bank, became the company's first executive director and later its president. Production began in late 1959. During the 1960s, the government sold off its interest to the private investors, and Japan Synthetic Rubber became unambiguously a type V national policy company.[37]

Another classic example of a type V company is the Kyōdō Oil Company. Petroleum has long been a strategic concern of the Japanese government, as it is of most governments. The Japanese case is complicated by the fact that during the occupation the Americans kept Japan dependent on the major American oil companies; and by the 1960s, Japan had become the world's largest petroleum importer. Watanabe Yōzō feels that for the decade after Japan regained its independence,

---

[37] Matsumura, *Japan's Economic Growth*, pp. 193-94.

the Americans held both a nuclear and a petroleum umbrella over Japan.[38]

There was not a great deal that Japan could do about prospecting and drilling for crude oil of its own, although in 1955 it did set up the Petroleum Resources Development Company (a re-creation in the postwar world of the Imperial Oil Company of 1941), which was a type II *tokushu kaisha*. In 1967, the company was elevated to the status of a *kōdan*. The company and later the *kōdan* supplied funds for overseas oil exploration to such type VI national policy companies as the Arabian Oil Company of Japan (created in 1958) and the North Sumatra Petroleum Development Company (created in 1960). On the domestic refining front, however, MITI was determined to break the hold of foreign interests if it possibly could. Throughout the 1950s the main Japanese refiners and distributors had foreign connections, and they often seemed, at least in Japanese government eyes, to serve foreign rather than national interests. (Tōa Nenryō was affiliated with Standard-Vacuum; Mitsubishi with Tidewater Associated; Nihon Sekiyu with Caltex; Shōwa Sekiyu with Shell; Kōa with Caltex; and Maruzen with Union Oil.) The ties between the Japanese firms and their American patrons were based on long-term sales contracts negotiated in 1949 at SCAP's insistence. Article 7(2) of the Japanese-American Treaty of Friendship and Commerce of 1953 further protected the rights already gained in Japan by the American oil firms. It should be noted, of course, that in 1949 Japan had no source of oil other than the U.S. Army, and the American firms that entered into these SCAP-initiated contracts had no notion that the Japanese market would grow so rapidly (and so profitably).

By the early 1960s, MITI felt that it had to do something about this situation. The Ikeda government had committed the country to trade liberalization, and the ministry feared that once the American oil companies got free access to Japan they would take over completely all domestic refining. MITI therefore enacted the Petroleum Industry Law in 1962, which was intended to prevent "excessive competition" in the petroleum importing, refining, and distributing business, and required that virtually every transaction concerning oil receive the approval of the minister of international trade and industry. In 1965, MITI went further and created Kyōdō Sekiyu K.K. (the Kyōdō Oil Company), based on the merger of Nippon Mining Company, Asia Oil

---

[38] Watanabe Yōzō, "Sekiyu sangyō to sengo keizaihō taisei" [The petroleum industry and the structure of postwar economic law], in Tōkyō Daigaku Shakai Kagaku Kenkyūjo [Tokyo University Social Science Research Institute], ed., *Sengo kaikaku* [Postwar reform] (Tokyo: Tokyo Daigaku Shakai Kagaku Kenkyūjo, 1975), vol. 8, p. 250.

56

Company, and Tōa Oil Company (later joined by the Kashima and Fuji oil companies), as a wholly Japanese-owned rival to the companies with foreign connections. The negotiations to establish the firm were directed by Saitō Hideo, then chief of the Petroleum Planning Section of MITI's Mining Bureau (in 1975 he was director general of the Patent Agency). The idea of creating Kyōdō Sekiyu was provided primarily by Hayashi Shintarō, one of MITI's few Ph.D.'s in economics.[39]

Under the leadership of Mori Chikao (MITI 1934–1959), who took over as Kyōdō's vice-president in October 1967 and became president in November 1969, the company grew in the face of stiff competition. In May 1974, Mori was succeeded as president by Koide Eiichi (MITI 1935–1962), who had retired as vice-minister of the Economic Planning Agency. By 1974, Kyōdō Oil had become Japan's largest independent oil company, with about 17 percent of the country's domestic refining capacity. Still, to foreign oil interests, Kyōdō is known not as a "Japanese major," which MITI had hoped it would become, but as a "MITI dummy."[40]

Following the oil shock of 1973, MITI proposed even further mergers of Japanese refiners and their integration with the overseas exploration companies. The whole system was to be controlled by the Japan Petroleum Development Corporation (Sekiyu Kaihatsu Kōdan), whose president in 1975 was Shimada Yoshito, a former chief of MITI's powerful Enterprises Bureau. This reorganization was still being studied during 1977.

Although Kyōdō Oil has not been financed by the government, it belongs to the type V national policy companies because of its origins in the offices of MITI. Its purpose always has been to further one of Japan's national economic policy goals: to ensure that Japan would not be totally dependent on foreigners for the refining and sale of the petroleum it must import.

National Policy Companies, Broadly Defined

The firms in our sixth category belong to a blurred area between enterprises launched by government initiative and purely private, even if government-regulated, businesses. These in-between firms are distinguished by having a high concentration of retired government bureaucrats

---

[39] Nihon Chōki Shin'yō Ginkō [Japan Long-Term Credit Bank], *Jūyō sangyō sengo nijūgo nenshi* [The history of important industries during the 25 postwar years] (Tokyo: Sangyō to Keizai, 1972), pp. 61-119; *Nihon keizai shimbun*, June 25, 1974, p. 9; *Daily Yomiuri*, September 14, 1975; *Japan Times*, May 2, 1974; and *Kōkyū kanryō sōran* (1971 ed.), pp. 152-53.

[40] *Asahi shimbun*, April 16, 1974, morning ed., p. 3.

on their boards of directors, strong delegations of their executives on powerful government advisory commissions, and a history of direct involvement with the government in forms such as governmental assistance at their births, administrative guidance, governmental subsidies, and governmental brokerage in effecting mergers or joint ventures. Type VI national policy companies are comparable to the defense industries in the United States. Often these firms have been singled out for governmental aid or protection, as distinct from governmental efforts to foster or protect their industry as a whole. The coal industry is certainly an object of national policy in Japan, but the private coal companies are not national policy companies. However, Arabian Oil and Alaska Pulp are national policy companies, as we have already seen. So are Fujitsū Computers and New Japan Steel.

In 1973, Amaya Naohiro of MITI wrote:

> The Japanese Government regards the computer industry as being as important to Japan as the defense industry to the United States. The American defense industry is protected by the Buy America Act and other institutions, and it is exempted from liberalization under GATT and the code of the OECD. . . . It has been judged that the computer industry is strategically important in the present and future industrial policy [of Japan]. . . . Computers produced in Japan by American subsidiaries and those imported from the United States already account for 46 percent of the Japanese market, and this share is high enough.[41]

During the 1970s, there were six purely Japanese computer manufacturers: Fujitsū, Hitachi, Mitsubishi Electric, Nippon Electric, Tōshiba, and Oki Electric. There were also five United States–based firms operating in Japan: IBM, Burroughs, Control Data, NCR, and Univac (the last is associated with Oki, which owns the majority share of their joint venture). IBM sells the most computers; Fujitsū is second. Fujitsū is the leading manufacturer of computers sold to the Japanese government. It also cooperates with Hitachi and Mitsubishi in accepting both guidance and subsidies from the government for research and development. Sales and rentals of its hardware are supported by the government's Japan Electronic Computer Company, and since January 1973, Akazawa Shōichi, former chief of MITI's Heavy Industry Bureau, has served as an adviser to the company. Fujitsū is, in short, Japan's primary instrument for the national attempt to compete successfully with IBM in the global computer market.

---

[41] Amaya Naohiro, "Imediate Economic Problems between Japan and the United States and Their Long-Range Prospects" (Tokyo: MITI Information Office, March 6, 1973), pp. 11-12.

58

An even clearer example of a type VI national policy company is the New Japan Steel Company, formed on March 31, 1970, by the merger of the Yawata and Fuji steel companies. Old trade and industry bureaucrats have a warm place in their hearts for Yawata Steel. Their connection with it dates back to the creation of the government-owned foundry at Yawata during the Meiji period, operated as a direct government enterprise until it was transformed into the Japan Steel Corporation in 1934. Even then, retired MCI officials continued to dominate its board of directors until SCAP divided it into two separate companies during the occupation. Japanese wits liked to describe MITI itself as the "Tokyo office of the Yawata Steel Company." The idea of reuniting Yawata and Fuji into Japan Steel was never far from the thoughts of MITI bureaucrats.

During the recession of 1965, beginning with the bankruptcy of Sanyō Special Steel, MITI launched a campaign to eliminate what it derided as Japan's "cherry blossom-viewing and sake-drinking economy" (hanamizake no keizai). What the economic officials meant by this wisecrack was that the key sectors of the Japanese economy were divided into too many low-equity, excessively invested firms to compete with the giant corporations of the United States and Germany on anything like equitable terms. They decided to promote large-scale mergers, with the intent of ending the cutthroat internal competition that existed at the time and preparing Japan to resist the threat of takeovers by foreign capital. MITI encouraged the merger of the three Mitsubishi Heavy Industries companies, of Nissan with Prince Motors, and of Tōyōbō with Kureha Spinning. Then, in tune with the logic of the times but also with the memory of past bureaucratic glory, MITI proposed the merger of Yawata and Fuji.

Yamamoto Shigenobu, MITI vice-minister between April 1966 and May 1968, personally conducted negotiations between Yawata president Inayama Yoshihiro and Fuji president Nagano Shigeo. He was greatly aided by Hirai Tomisaburō, a former MITI vice-minister (1953–1955), who was on the board of directors at Yawata, and Tokunaga Hizatsugu, a former MITI vice-minister (1960–1961), on the board of directors at Fuji. As a consequence of the merger, Hirai moved up to become vice-president of New Japan Steel (he became president in May 1973), and Tokunaga became the third-ranking executive director (senmu). Within the ministry, Yamamoto was backed up by Yoshimitsu Hisashi, chief of the Heavy Industry Bureau from 1968 to 1969 (and after retirement a director of the Development Bank), and Sakon Tomosaburō, chief of the bureau's Iron and Steel Business Section (Tekkō Gyōmu-ka) from 1966 to 1969 (and in 1974 chief of the General Affairs Section of the Secretariat).

After an eighteen-month campaign and the hammering out of a compromise that the Fair Trade Commission would accept, Yamamoto and his colleagues were able to announce the government's approval of the merger on October 30, 1969. The following year New Japan Steel came into being. It is Japan's largest enterprise and the world's largest steel producer. Although this merger was supported by leaders of the two firms and other "seniors" of the *zaikai,* it was also a matter of government policy—and of MITI nostalgia; to fail to recognize this is to miss one of the vital nuances of Japanese industrial life.[42]

Conclusions

We have spanned a huge range of economic, political, and social activities in attempting to relate industries as diverse as the Japanese postal service (a direct government enterprise) and New Japan Steel (a major private corporation of concern to the government). Moreover, beyond the obvious national policy industries, such as computers, steel, electric power, automobiles, and shipbuilding, there exists a world of big business toward which the government is by no means indifferent. Our six categories, however, constitute those types of corporations that may reasonably be described as public policy companies, ranging from the companies with the most direct government connections to those with only tenuous connections. Along this spectrum, it is the 112 special legal entities of type II that are of primary interest in this study, since they have the clearest public corporate character. But it is important to remember, as this typology has sought to drive home, that the idea of "public corporation" in Japan is a range of alternatives, not a neat, legal pigeonhole.

[42] Shigen Kaihatsu Un'ei Chōsakai, ed., *Zaikaijin jiten* [Dictionary of business leaders] (Tokyo: Shigen Kaihatsu Un'ei Chōsakai, 1973), p. 32; and Nawa, *Tsūsan-shō,* pp. 42-43. Some sources hold that Ojima Arakazu was the true source of inspiration behind the merger. He was an MCI bureaucrat from 1918 to 1941, when he resigned as MCI vice-minister and entered Japan Steel. By 1943 he was vice-president of the company. After the war he continued with Yawata, becoming president in January 1956. In May 1967 he ascended to the role of "counselor" *(sodan-yaku)* at Yawata. But as Shiba and Nozue remark, "[A] *sodan-yaku* is not merely consulted. In fact, no major decision is ever made without his consent" (Shiba Kimpei, and Nozue Kenzo, *What Makes Japan Tick* [Tokyo: Asahi Evening News Co., 1971], p. 20). Ojima was never seen in negotiation between Yawata president Inayama and Fuji president Nagano, but he is said to have pushed the merger with all his influence. His career provides a direct link between (old) Japan Steel and New Japan Steel—and between the two of them and MITI.

60

3

Origins

The public corporation is one manifestation of government's attempts, and success, at state control of the economy. Its origins in Japan lie in the rise there of the control ideology. In general, state interventions in economic affairs take innumerable forms, from indirect taxes and tariffs to government's direct operation of productive facilities. However, the results of such interventions depend in large part on the political and economic values of the managers and workers who are on the receiving end of intervention. As J. P. Nettl argues:

> [A] distinction should be made between the notion of an industrial society, which is perfectly capable of development under the aegis of state-dominated social goal-attainment for nationalistic purposes, and a consumer-oriented society where industrialization is primarily related to, and concerned with, the satisfaction of individual consumption wants. Both are forms of industrialization, but the former is capable of being dominated by the state—indeed, the Soviet model provides the preeminent case of state guidance for industrialization without dominant consumer perspectives, and similar orientations can be deduced from the industrializing philosophy of late nineteenth-century Japan, Germany, and even Russia. But a mass consumption society—and particularly its cultural structuring right through society to the working classes—may not be a suitable or successful context for a dominant state. In societies with such goals, the state may be confined to regulating conflicting interests and possibly to the provision of the complementary infrastructure of education, road-building, nature conservation, public utilities, and so on.[1]

---

[1] J. P. Nettl, "The State as a Conceptual Variable," *World Politics*, vol. 20, no. 4 (July 1968), p. 587, n. 44.

State intervention has been tried in both state-dominated and consumer-oriented societies. Its success, however, has varied, partly depending on how well the government attempting to gain control has chosen a method that accords with the society's values. In one country, nationalization may have gratifying results; in another, indicative planning may work better. Both productivity and the legitimacy of the state's control are affected by the forms of intervention chosen and the reputation and skill of the state officials designated to administer them.

The ideology of state economic control has been on the rise in *all* economies since the 1930s. Nonetheless, even in states whose economic problems were originally more or less equivalent (overcoming the depression, mobilizing for war production, and so on) and whose ideologies included comparable goals (equity, planning, growth), the results both to the institutions attempting control and to the economies' performance have differed widely. The reason, of course, is that the details of history make bigger differences than comparativists usually imagine.

State intervention in the Japanese economy from approximately 1930 to 1960 looks vaguely similar to that in the United States, England, Germany, France, and Italy during the same period. In all of these countries, government intervened to rationalize the industrial structure and to direct capital where it would do the most to overcome the depression; all mobilized for war preparation and war production. Thus all found themselves tolerating (or saddled with) greater state economic activity in 1960 than had existed in 1930. But their detailed histories and political preconceptions differ markedly—and so do the lessons they have drawn from their histories for the postwar period.

From the Meiji Restoration to the Allied occupation, Japan was what Nettl describes as the state-dominated type of industrial society. For about two decades after 1868, the Meiji leaders attempted to engage directly in industrial enterprise, despite their lack of experience at it and the corruption and bureaucratism it generated. After that time they turned to supporting those businessmen who seemed to have the greatest chance of being successful. By the end of the Meiji era, many government-supported and government-protected businesses could and wanted to stand on their own. But the government never completely withdrew from involvement in commerce and industry. As John Roberts writes with regard to Mitsui,

[The firm's] government-related business was no longer a decisive factor [around 1910]: the concern had now become capable of sustained and flexible growth with self-generated capital. It was then, if ever, that this eminently respectable

62

organization could have reasserted its independence and become a private enterprise in the international sense. Yet while Mitsui's businessmen had been trying to create a structure that could stand alone, Inoue Kaoru and his fellow oligarchs, still regarding Mitsui as an instrument of national policy, had been tightening the cords of gold and silver that bound it to the state.[2]

Byron Marshall has shown in persuasive detail how small a foothold the ideology of entrepreneurial independence and consumer satisfaction had in prewar Japan. "No Japanese entrepreneur," he writes, "is recorded as having claimed the right to run his enterprise as he saw fit without outside intervention."[3]

And yet, during World War II, Marshall concludes, "Despite the elaborate administrative structure that existed on paper during the war years, neither effective centralization nor bureaucratic control was ever fully implemented."[4] This view is shared by virtually every analyst who has studied the period. Wartime Japan was an authoritarian but never a totalitarian society; in fact, the United States came much closer to producing total mobilization for the war effort than Japan ever did. The explanation for this anomaly lies in the fact that although Japan had a history of state intervention in the Meiji period, this changed from about the time of the Russo-Japanese War. As a new class of more independent industrial capitalists came to the fore, the state actually withdrew from economic management, except for maintaining contacts with major zaibatsu such as Mitsui. This was a period when more state and zaibatsu interests were situated overseas than in Japan proper. Twenty years later, when conditions forced state policies for the domestic economy to change, government again moved toward taking a role in the economy. The form this renewed state intervention took became intensely controversial and a focus for resistance among the various groups of industrialists. The state never achieved a total victory over them before Japan itself was defeated in 1945.

Only during the occupation did the state finally gain hegemony over private economic interests. Even then, the heritage of resistance to bureaucratic control, combined with the economic ideology of the Americans, dictated that state economic activity would take the form of public corporations and mixed public-private enterprises rather than direct control by economic ministries. These public corporate forms

---

2 John G. Roberts, *Mitsui* (Tokyo: Weatherhill, 1973), p. 186.

3 Byron K. Marshall, *Capitalism and Nationalism in Prewar Japan* (Stanford, Calif.: Stanford University Press, 1967), p. 75.

4 Ibid., p. 111.

had been legitimated by their use before and during the war. Japan is certainly a type of political economy conducive to state intervention; still, the state's role has had to be negotiated and both bureaucrats and businessmen have learned valuable lessons from their earlier, bitter experiences in trying to work with each other.

Early Origins: The Prewar Period

There were three general causes for Japanese demands for state intervention in the economy during the late 1920s and 1930s. First was the economic depression that had persisted in Japan throughout the decade following World War I, a depression deepened and exacerbated by the financial panic of 1927 and the world economic crisis of 1929. Second was the growing opposition to monopoly capitalism by idealistic and highly nationalistic military officers and by the victims of economic exploitation. Particularly after the zaibatsu's speculative dollar buying between June 1930 and December 1931, in anticipation of Japan's leaving gold convertibility, criticism of big business and demands for the nationalization of key industries became a major social movement. Third was the requirements of war production and rationing as Japan went to war in China in 1937 and throughout the Pacific area in 1941.[5]

In the face of these problems, all groups in the society agreed that some form of government action was necessary; but they never agreed on what form this action should take. Industrialists in general, and the zaibatsu in particular, favored what they called *jishu tōsei,* or self-control. This meant government would approve cartels in all important industries and give them legal support against outsiders. These cartels were treaty-like arrangements among established firms to control prices, production, and the terms of trade for a whole industry. Ever since the Exporter's Association Law of 1925, the government had favored this approach to trying to end cutthroat competition and dumping among small exporters and medium and small enterprises. With the onset of the Great Depression, big business asked that the cartels be extended to their sectors. The zaibatsu wanted the cartels in order to bring competitors under their own control; they saw them as stepping stones to takeovers and mergers. The government favored cartels as instruments of rationalization—that is, ways of reducing excess competition and making Japan's industrial structure more like that of its international competitors. Independent or new zaibatsu businesses were suspicious of the cartels, but they accepted them because cartels afforded some

---

[5] See Nakamura Takafusa, *Nihon no keizai tōsei* [Japan's economic controls] (Tokyo: Nikkei Shinsho No. 208, 1974), pp. 23-29.

64

defense against old zaibatsu encroachments, and because they were, in the last analysis, preferable to outright nationalization. Thus *jishu tōsei,* meaning cartelization, was inaugurated among the big businesses in Japan proper with the enactment of the Important Industries Control Law in 1931.[6]

The military and those civilian bureaucrats who subscribed to what in the 1930s was called the *kakushin* ("reform") persuasion preferred *kokka tōsei,* or state control. *Kakushin* in this context was actually a euphemism for support of European fascism, Soviet-type economic planning, and totalitarianism. At a minimum *kokka tōsei* meant the sort of commodity and price controls that England and Germany had enforced during World War I. It further implied the use of state authority to control prices, quantities, terms, and productive facilities, normally through elaborate regulations and plans.

The first major Japanese attempt to put such state control into operation occurred in colonized Manchuria under the supervision of the Kwantung Army and the Economic Research Association of the South Manchurian Railroad. The Japanese leaders of Manchuria were intensely opposed to the zaibatsu on the grounds that such monopoly capitalists were corrupting the political life of Japan and putting their own profits ahead of what the militarists took to be Japan's destiny. Underlying this anticapitalist bias was their serious military concern that Japan had never experienced a total mobilization for war such as the European powers had during World War I. The military and the *kakushin kanryō* ("reform bureaucrats") recognized that Japan did not have the industrial might necessary for modern warfare, and they wanted to build it rapidly. During the 1930s, they were also excited by the Soviet Union's first and second five-year plans—both by the plans' orientation toward war-related industrial development and by their construction in terms of commodities rather than money.[7]

---

[6] One of the most useful articles on this topic is Takase Masao, "Nihon ni okeru dokusen kiseihō no keifu" [The genealogy of monopoly regulation legislation in Japan], *Hōritsu jihō,* vol. 46, no. 1 (January 1974), pp. 76-87.

[7] Philip H. Trezise is simply mistaken when he writes, "As with many of the institutions and procedures in Japan's postwar economic policymaking, the elaboration of formal national economic plans had its origin in the American occupation" ("Politics, Government, and Economic Growth in Japan," in H. Patrick and H. Rosovsky, eds., *Asia's New Giant* [Washington, D.C.: Brookings Institution, 1976], p. 789). Japanese national planning had its origins during the 1930s in Manchuria and after the outbreak of the Sino-Japanese war in Japan proper. For works on prewar and wartime planning, see Inaba Hidezō, *Gekidō sanjūnen no Nihon keizai* [Thirty years of upheaval in the Japanese economy] (Tokyo: Jitsugyō no Nihon Sha, 1965); Nakamura, *Nihon no keizai tōsei;* and Tanaka Shin'ichi, *Nihon senji keizai hishi* [Secret history of Japan's wartime economy] (Tokyo: Computer Age Co., 1974). Both Tanaka and Inaba were senior economic

As it turned out, the Manchurian experimenters failed on their own terms and had to turn to private industrialists for assistance. They both avoided and were rebuffed by the old-line zaibatsu (Mitsui, Mitsubishi, Yasuda, and Sumitomo), at least at first; instead they turned to the so-called new zaibatsu, industrialists such as Ayukawa Gisuke of Nissan, who was both friendly to the military and in competition with the established zaibatsu. As these two groups, facists and pro-military industrialists, sought a way to work with each other to develop Japan's new continental holdings, they turned to the joint public-private enterprise as the appropriate instrument. They called it a *kokusaku kaisha,* or national policy company.

At the same time that the Manchurian radicals were using the public corporation to implement state control of the economy, different but comparable struggles were coming to a head in Japan proper. Before the creation of the Japan Steel Corporation in 1934, there were very few special legal entities or national policy companies in Japan. Those that did exist were involved almost exclusively in colonial development. The main ones were the Nippon Kangyō Bank (established in 1897), the Bank of Taiwan (1899), the Hokkaido Development Bank (1900), the Industrial Bank of Japan (1902), the South Manchurian Railroad Company (1906), the Oriental Development Company (1908; it operated primarily in Korea), the Yalu River Extraction and Lumber Company (1908), the Bank of Korea (1909), the Japan-Russia Fishing Company (1914), the Korea Industrial Bank (1918), Taiwan Electric Power (1919), and a few others.[8] Only in Yalu River Extraction and the South Manchurian Railroad did the government own a majority of the shares. Both of the companies set up in 1926 for mining and oil drilling in North Sakhalin were zaibatsu affiliates; they did not receive government funds, but they were considered national policy companies because they received government guarantees and supervision and because the government assisted them in international exchange transactions.

---

planning officials in the government during the late 1930s and the war. Concerning economic planning by the military in Manchuria, see Mark R. Peattie, *Ishiwara Kanji and Japan's Confrontation with the West* (Princeton: Princeton University Press, 1975), pp. 208-19.

Trezise is similarly in error when he remarks, "One of Japan's inheritances from the American occupation is the institution of public committees and councils in an advisory capacity to the government" (p. 769), and refers to "the advisory councils, *shingikai,* inherited from the American occupation" (p. 785). Advisory councils actually go back to the middle of the Meiji period. For a list of some 34 advisory committees attached to the prewar Ministry of Commerce and Industry alone, see Shōkō Gyōsei Chōsa Kai, ed., *Shōkō-shō yōran* [Ministry of Commerce and Industry handbook] (Tokyo: Shōkō Gyōsei Sha, 1941), pp. 79-154.

[8] Noda Keizai Kenkyūjo, *Senjika no kokusaku kaisha* [National policy companies during wartime] (Tokyo: Noda Keizai Kenkyūjo, 1940), pp. 67-106, 690.

The first true domestic *kokusaku kaisha* was Japan Steel. Although the company was anything but typical of the numerous national policy companies that followed it, because of government's long-time involvement in steel manufacturing, its creation in 1934 gave major impetus to the use of the public corporate form as a compromise between the advocates of self-control and the advocates of state control. Japan Steel's origins go back to World War I. At that time there was a great increase in the number of private steel companies, and an expansion of the government-operated steel works at Yawata, because of the war boom. This led to an excess of steel-making capacity that plagued the industry throughout the 1920s. To overcome these problems, and also to deal with recurrent corruption and conflicts of interest in the operation of the Yawata works, the idea was advanced as early as 1924 that all of Japan's steel facilities should be amalgamated into one public-private concern. The time to act on this idea finally arrived during the Saitō cabinet of 1932, when the government launched its programs of military expansion and the arguments against bailing out depressed private steel makers at public expense were no longer valid.

In short, Japan Steel (created by law 47 of April 6, 1933) was the result not so much of the state's effort to bring the civilian economy under control, since the state's position in steel was already dominant, as of the desire of most parties concerned to rationalize the steel industry. Japan Steel also differed from the Manchurian national policy companies in that it did not come to occupy a monopoly position in the steel industry; some prominent firms, such as Nippon Kōkan, refused to join.[9] Still, as a successful example of state-private cooperation (the first president of Japan Steel, Nakai Reisaku, had been an MCI bureaucrat from 1903 to 1934), it provided an important precedent in Japan proper for attempts to duplicate the Manchurian companies.

In the years immediately following the establishment of Japan Steel, the militarists and the industrialists argued publicly and violently about the nature and degree of state economic control that Japan needed. In this great debate the civilian economic bureaucracies were split between "reform bureaucrats" allied with the military and traditional bureaucrats allied with big business. Although the contrast is perhaps drawn too sharply, Shiroyama Saburō argues that Yoshino Shinji (MCI vice-minister from December 1931 to October 1936 and minister from June 1937 to May 1938) was the most important bureaucratic advocate of self-control, while Kishi Nobusuke (MCI vice-

---

[9] On the ways in which Shiraishi Motojirō, the founder and president of Nippon Kōkan, resisted the pressures to join Japan Steel, see Miki Yōnosuke, *Keizai jiken no shuyaku-tachi* [Leading personalities of the economic scandals] (Tokyo: Sankei Shimbun, 1968), pp. 54-61.

minister from October 1939 to January 1941, minister from October 1941 to October 1943, and vice-minister of munitions from November 1943 to July 1944) was the most important bureaucratic advocate of state control.[10]

The crucial point today about the whole debate is that neither side ever saw its position completely prevail. For various complex reasons that need to be only mentioned here—including army-navy rivalries, technical inexperience on the part of military and civilian planners, and above all a commitment by industrial and zaibatsu leaders to the principle of private property—Japan's war economy remained "semi-private." The Japanese government moved toward state control, but not until June and July 1945 did the militarists and bureaucrats actually succeed in taking over private factories. By then it was too late to affect production, and the industrialists were glad when the government paid to nationalize their now profitless businesses.[11]

National Policy Companies and Control Associations

The advocates of European-style fascism in the bureaucracy tried throughout the war to introduce totalitarianism to Japan. However, as they realized that their opponents were too powerful and too entrenched to be overcome (Kobayashi Ichizō, MCI minister when Kishi was vice-minister, once denounced his leading subordinate as a crypto-Communist because of his advocacy of state control), they turned to the state corporation as the best available alternative. Two forms of government-influenced corporation emerged from this movement. The first was the national policy companies, modeled not so much on Japan Steel as on Aiyukawa Gisuke's Manchurian Heavy Industries Development Corporation (Manshū Jūkōgyō Kaihatsu K.K.), set up in 1937 after the Kwantung Army had given up on its goal of direct economic control. Employing for various periods such "reform bureaucrats" as Kishi and Shiina Etsusaburō of the MCI, Aiyukawa's company controlled 18 satellite companies and 130 subcontracting companies, and it held a monopoly over all manufacturing in Manchuria. The second result of the movement toward public corporations was the "control associations" (tōseikai), which were really the old self-control cartels of 1931, with the government now providing some of the top management.

---

[10] Shiroyama Saburō, "Tsūsan kanryō jinbutsu shōshi" [A short history of the personalities in the trade and industry bureaucracy], Chūō kōron, August 1975, p. 306.
[11] Roberts, Mitsui, p. 362; Tsūshō Sangyō-shō Daijin Kanbō Chōsa-ka [MITI Secretariat, Research Section], Tsūshō sangyō-shō shijūnen shi [Forty-year history of MITI] (Tokyo: Tsūsan Shiryō Chōsa Kai, 1965), p. 382.

The main late-1930s national policy companies were the Imperial Oil Company (founded in 1941), the Japan Power Generation and Distribution Company (1938), the Imperial Mining Development Company (1939), the Great Japan Aircraft Company (1939), the Japan Coal Company (1939), the Petroleum Cooperative Sales Company (1939), and many others set up in China. All were joint public-private "special companies." At the time they were coming into being, most leftist Japanese critics and virtually all foreign analysts denounced them as manifestations of capitalistic munitions makers' promoting Japan's foreign wars in order to swallow up smaller competitors and reap huge profits under the cover of patriotism. Whether or not this was true, these national policy companies also signified a degree of success in the Japanese industrial world's resistance against much more radical plans for full totalitarian control. Moreover, even though the new companies served zaibatsu interests, they also contributed to the rationalization of Japanese industry by reducing the excessively large number of firms, by concentrating the capital needed for heavy and chemical industrialization, and by providing training grounds for the managers and bureaucrats who led Japan's economy during the 1950s to its unprecedented growth.

A good example of such a company is the Japan Express Company (Nihon Tsūun K.K.), which by 1957 had become the key land transportation firm in the country. In that year it moved some 230 million tons of merchandise throughout Japan—nearly half of all goods transported by truck, and well above the total of 160 million tons of freight carried by the Japan National Railways. Japan Express is a product of the craze for national policy companies and mergers that swept Japan between 1937 and 1941. Created by a special law in 1937, with the government putting up part of the capital, it merged six firms, including the well-known International Transportation Company (Kokusai Un'yu K.K.). In 1941 Japan Express absorbed another fifty-six small express companies, and competition in the trucking business disappeared. In 1949, the occupation authorities ordered the Japan Express Company Law repealed, and the firm became a truly private, commercial corporation. In 1957, some 42 percent of its shares were held by banks, 48 percent by individuals, 5 percent by securities companies, 3 percent by the government and public corporations, and 2 percent by private corporations. It had become a typical type VI national policy company.[12]

---

[12] Supreme Commander for the Allied Powers, Monograph 25, "Deconcentration of Economic Power," *Historical Monographs* (Washington, D.C.: National Archives, 1951), p. 57; and Matsumura Yutaka, *Japan's Economic Growth 1945–1960* (Tokyo: Tokyo News Service, 1961), pp. 340-41.

Mixed public-private enterprises like Japan Express met some of Japan's wartime needs, but the militarists and bureaucrats were dissatisfied. They were irritated by the fact that the national policy companies continued to pay interest and dividends to private capitalists during a period of national emergency, even though the dividends were not large. (The highest rates were paid by Japan Steel, the Kangyō Bank, and Japan-Russia Fishing—about 10 percent. The Korea Industrial Bank paid 9 percent, the South Manchurian Railroad a high of 8 percent on public shares, and all others 7 percent or less.) The national policy companies met another nationalist demand by limiting ownership of their shares to citizens or legal entities of the empire; but they were still criticized for being zaibatsu-dominated. The laws establishing the companies usually stipulated that the government would name the president and vice-president, but the zaibatsu firms supplied most of the other personnel. They did this partly to maintain control and to compete with each other, but also because the official bureaucrats lacked the necessary technical and managerial skills to run such companies. As far as can be determined, the first use of the term *amakudari* ("descent from heaven") to refer to bureaucrats' practice of retiring early and taking lucrative jobs on the boards of directors of national policy companies occurred in the Diet in 1937, when it was suggested that some national policy companies were being set up primarily for that purpose.[13] Even so, the presence of a few ex-bureaucrats did not ensure state control. Today, both the term *amakudari* and the practice are commonplaces of the Japanese political system.

As part of their pressure toward a more tightly controlled "national defense state," the militarists promoted the passage of the National General Mobilization Law in 1938. This law was written by military and civilian officials of the Cabinet Planning Board; it was a comprehensive mobilization statute intended to cover every war production requirement by controlling labor, the establishment of new companies, additions to capital, mergers, changes of product, and so forth. To get the law passed by the Diet, however, the military had to make it merely authorizing legislation; all details of implementation were left to imperial ordinances. The mobilization law is the benchmark of the beginning of government's authority to conduct investigations of businesses, demand reports, and engage in administrative guidance, activities that have flourished to this day.

Article 17 of the National General Mobilization Law realized the second part of the militarists' move toward state control through public corporations. This article authorized the formation of cartels in indus-

---

13 Noda Keizai Kenkyūjo, *Senjika no kokusaku kaisha*, p. 59.

tries for the purpose of coming to "control agreements" (*tōsei kyōtei*); it was thus the legal basis for the later "control associations." Every attempt to implement the law, however, produced bitter disputes within the government and the Diet. Even the cabinet's decision at the end of 1940 to adopt the "Outline Plan for the Establishment of the New Economic Structure" did not silence industrialists' charges that the military and the bureaucracy were infiltrated by "reds." Not until August 30, 1941, with global war almost a reality, was the government able to implement article 17. It did so through the Important Industries Association Ordinance (Imperial Ordinance 831), which ordered the creation of control associations (*tōseikai*) throughout industry. In October, Tōjō's new Minister of Commerce and Industry, Kishi Nobusuke, made the first designations under the ordinance, directing twelve sectors of the economy—steel, coal, mining, cement, electrical machinery, automobiles, and six other major industries—to form themselves into control associations. The following July the second designations were made, and by the end of the war there were about 2,000 control associations, covering every industry and economic transaction in Japan.

The control associations were actually the old cartels of 1931 and thereafter, now upgraded, expanded, and made official governmental organs. Under the terms of the Transfer of Administrative Authority Law of 1942, the directors of the control associations became quasi-governmental officials, and their orders carried the force of law. Takahashi Makoto writes:

A kind of compulsory cartel to fulfill production quotas, carry out assignments regarding materials and labor, and the like, the control associations were empowered as agencies of state authority to exercise compulsory control over individual enterprises. . . .They were also endowed with authority as a sort of state organ directly belonging to either the Ministry of Commerce and Industry or the Munitions Ministry. On the other hand, however, these institutions were operated by representatives of the major zaibatsu, and virtually conducted on the principle of securing the interests of the zaibatsu.[14]

The Cabinet Planning Board and the Ministry of Commerce and Industry set production targets for each industry, based on government's so-called materials mobilization plans, and then passed the targets to the control associations for implementation. The Important Industries Association Ordinance also brought all forms of distribution under control and created joint sales companies for the products of all firms in a given

[14] Takahashi Makoto, "The Development of Wartime Economic Controls," *The Developing Economies,* vol. 5, no. 4 (December 1967), p. 663.

71

industry. Prices were controlled by the Price Control Ordinance of 1939. Each firm thus belonged to many different control associations— one for its industry, one for raw materials, one for sales, and so on. Japan Steel, for example, belonged to or participated in twenty-four different control associations.[15]

Despite the totalitarian ambitions of the drafters of the law and the ordinance, the control associations were anything but what they hoped to create. Itō Mitsuharu recalls:

> Control associations appeared in each industry and created their own control agencies. Managers of the major industrial enterprises were appointed to represent their industries: for example, the head of the Cement Control Association was president of Asano Cement, the head of the Mining Control Association was president of Nihon Mining, and so on. The allotment of production quotas, apportionment of materials, determination of prices, and distribution of profits were left up to these associations. On the orders of those associations, small enterprises were forced to supply labor for large enterprises; the associations functioned, in effect, to support and build up big enterprises at the expense of the small, which were consequently drained.[16]

T. A. Bisson notes another unintended consequence:

> During 1940–41 the zaibatsu won their fight for the ordinance establishing the Control Associations as the administrative organs of industrial mobilization in the "big war" seen to be approaching. When the war came these Industrial Control Associations, which were merely the private zaibatsu cartels under another name, proved thoroughly incapable of doing more than competing with each other for scarce commodities—a process which threw Japan's war economy into near chaos by the end of 1942.[17]

No one in an official position in the Japanese government at the time, least of all Prime Minister Tōjō or Minister of Commerce and Industry Kishi, would have disputed these assessments. They were quite aware that the tōseikai were zaibatsu-dominated and that they were not so much controlling industry as reorganizing it to suit their own interests. Thus, as the war situation worsened and the performance

---

[15] SCAP, Monograph 47, "The Heavy Industries," *Historical Monographs*, p. 22.

[16] Itō Mitsuharu, "Munitions Unlimited—The Controlled Economy," *The Japan Interpreter*, vol. 7, nos. 3-4 (Summer–Autumn 1972), p. 362.

[17] T. A. Bisson, *Japan's War Economy* (New York: Institute of Pacific Relations, 1945), p. x.

of the control associations became less tolerable, Tōjō and Kishi made one more effort to establish the kind of full state control they had sought for so many years. On November 1, 1943, they created the Ministry of Munitions, with Tōjō as minister (and concurrently prime minister) and Kishi as vice-minister. Under this new structure, the Cabinet Planning Board and the MCI were merged into the Ministry of Munitions' key organ, the General Mobilization Bureau, which put planning and top management in one agency. The Munitions Ministry also ordered state bureaucrats, either civilian or military, sent directly into the factories to see that production targets were being met.

But the new structure came too late to do much good. It merely placed another echelon of officials on top of the control associations (now called munitions companies); in spite of it, the cartels survived Japan's defeat and existed well into the occupation period. One further reason why the structure never worked very well was that the army and navy, recognizing the weaknesses of the cartels, went into direct production for themselves in their own armories and refineries, thus competing with the control companies for labor and materials.

Perhaps the best example of a control association is the first one— the Iron and Steel Control Association (Tekkō Tōseikai), established by MCI Notification 1082 of November 1941. It united forty-nine Japanese and Manchurian steel companies, including the big four of the Japanese steel industry: Japan Steel, Nippon Kōkan, Kawasaki Heavy Industries, and Kobe Steel. The president was Hirao Hachisaburō, the former president of the Kawasaki Shipbuilding Company, a director of Japan Steel, former president of Nichi-nan Sangyō K.K. (a national policy company in charge of financing Japanese emigration to Brazil),[18] and minister of education in the Hirota cabinet of 1936. Hirao was a figurehead; below him was a board of directors made up of a chairman, six directors, three auditors, and twenty-five "councillors" (hyōgiin) representing the most important member firms. On the operating side of the association were such later-famous industrialists as Nagano Shigeo (head of the tōseikai's Materials Department and postwar president of Fuji Steel), Inayama Yoshihiro (head of the Manufactured Products Department and later president of Yawata Steel), and Fujii Heigo (head of the General Affairs Department and

---

18 The first Japanese emigrants sailed for Brazil in 1908. In 1937 the government created Nichi-nan Sangyō to promote such emigration. After the war, in 1955, the government recreated it under the name of Japan Overseas Emigration Promotion Company, a wholly government-owned tokushu kaisha, controlled by the Ministry of Foreign Affairs. In 1963 it was upgraded to a jigyōdan and in 1974 merged with another jigyōdan to become part of the International Cooperation Agency, itself a newly created jigyōdan. Both the prewar and postwar public enterprises lent money to emigrants to cover their costs of travel and settlement.

after the war vice-minister of the Economic Stabilization Board created by the occupation authorities, a member of the House of Councillors, and vice-president of Yawata Steel). Rather than an organization to promote and control war production, this *tōseikai* was a trade association dominated by big business and with good governmental connections.[19]

The Eidan

One other group of wartime organizations must be mentioned because it provided precedents for the true state-dominated companies that came into being during the occupation. These were the seven *eidan* (literally, "business unit"). The most important *eidan* were the Important Materials Control Corporation (Jūyō Busshi Kanri Eidan), established in April 1942, a strategic materials stockpiling and warehousing organization; the Trade Corporation (Kōeki Eidan), begun in July 1943, which incorporated the Important Materials Control Corporation and expanded its duties to include, among other things, looting the Japanese occupied areas; and the Industrial Facilities Corporation (Sangyō Setsubi Eidan), set up in December 1941, which bought up and transferred machinery and equipment from nonessential industries to war-related industries.[20] The *eidan* had the status of wholly government-owned and government-managed special legal entities charged with functions that were difficult to perform on a private, profit-making basis, including control of the circulation of goods. They served to some extent to control the *tōseikai* by regulating their supplies. The military supported the *eidan* because they excluded zaibatsu financial or managerial influence.

Thus, at the end of the war the structure of governmental control in the Japanese economy comprised three layers: the General Mobilization Bureau of the Ministry of Munitions, the *eidan,* and the control associations. The government perpetuated this structure after the war by transforming the General Mobilization Bureau into the Economic Stabilization Board, the *eidan* into official government agencies such as the Board of Trade (Bōeki-chō) and the Coal Agency, and the control associations into genuine public corporations like the *eidan* but now known as *kōdan.*

---

[19] Komiyama Toshimasa, *Tōseikai to zaibatsu* (Tokyo: Kagaku-shugi Kōgyō Sha, 1942), pp. 69-72; *Tōseikai nenkan* [Control associations yearbook] (Tokyo: Itō Shoten, 1943), part 2, pp. 1-19; and Chōsa Shiryō Kyōkai, *Naigai chōsa shiryō,* vol. 14, no. 5 (July 1942), pp. 3-11, 67-71.

[20] MITI, *Tsūshō sangyō-shō shijūnen shi,* pp. 295, 298, 302.

The Occupation: State Control Accomplished

In the course of carrying out their duties, the Allied occupation authorities gave to the civilian Japanese bureaucracy the powers that had eluded it for almost a decade under Tōjō and Kishi.[21] MacArthur and his men did not, of course, intend to perpetuate the control associations. But when they found that they could not do without them and still maintain the economic controls that were desperately needed in a war-devastated country, they took the logical course of reforming and strengthening them. SCAP greatly increased the public character of the *tōseikai*, put them firmly under the control of central government ministries, and renamed them *kōdan*. In so doing, the Allies created the prototypes of the postwar special legal entities.[22] Occupation officials have only rarely acknowledged any continuity between the wartime and postwar economic control structure, and they seemed to think (or pretended) that they had introduced something new to Japan.[23] But the bureaucrats who controlled the *kōdan* knew better; they knew that with the break-up of the zaibatsu, the elimination of the military, and the strengthening of government controls over the public corporations, they had been provided with instruments to carry out their economic plans that were infinitely more effective than the *tōseikai*. State control finally triumphed over self-control in Japan during 1946.[24]

When MacArthur set up his headquarters in Tokyo in September 1945, he faced some difficult choices. Many of the orders and policy statements given to him by his superiors, as well as the views of mem-

---

[21] See Chalmers Johnson, "Japan: Who Governs? An Essay on Official Bureaucracy," *The Journal of Japanese Studies*, vol. 2, no. 1 (Autumn 1975), pp. 1-28.

[22] Note Watanabe Yasuo's comment: "The [postwar] special legal entities are a direct result of wartime controls, when the various control associations came into being. Prior to the Pacific War there were actually very few special legal entities. From the carrying out of the controlled economy immediately after the war, followed by monopoly enterprises, cooperative enterprises, and service enterprises, innumerable more were set up" ("Kōmuin no kyaria" [Careers of public officials], in Tsuji Kiyoaki, ed., *Gyōseigaku kōza* [Lectures on the science of public administration] [Tokyo: Tokyo Daigaku Shuppankai, 1976], vol. 4, p. 201).

[23] Note Jerome B. Cohen's observation, "The wartime control system with its vestiges of cartel domination was abolished, but the substitute allocation system had a very familiar appearance" (*Japan's Economy in War and Reconstruction* [Minneapolis: University of Minnesota Press, 1949], p. 431). Also see SCAP, "Elimination of Private Control Association," *Historical Monographs*, vol. 10, part C, passim. On the attempt by SCAP to suppress this monograph, see Johnson, *Journal of Japanese Studies*, p. 17, n. 46.

[24] Maeda Yasuyuki, writing in an official MITI journal, argues, "Direct control of commodities by the government occurred for the first time in August 1946" ("Tsūshō sangyō seisaku no rekishi-teki tenkai" [The historical development of trade and industrial policy], *Tsūsan jyānaru*, May 25, 1975, p. 11).

75

bers of his own staff, reflected the then current neo-Marxist ideology that wars in general, including the Pacific War, were caused by capitalist munitions makers. MacArthur thus was ordered to abolish the Japanese government's wartime economic controls, which were considered obstacles to the development of a "democratic economy" as well as former instruments of zaibatsu war-mongering and exploitation. But because the Japanese economy was in much worse shape than American planners had realized, SCAP was forced to direct the Japanese government— through which the Americans had chosen to carry out their program of reform, rather than attempt to undertake it themselves—to maintain wage and price controls and to institute an equitable rationing system.

On August 26, 1945, the day before the first Allied soldier arrived in Japan, the Japanese government, anticipating problems in the economic area but hoping to keep some control in its own hands, abolished the Ministry of Munitions and re-created the Ministry of Commerce and Industry. (The MCI lasted until 1949, when it was replaced by MITI.) This had the effect of abolishing the planning and coordinating agency of the wartime control system—the General Mobilization Bureau of the Ministry of Munitions—and leaving the control associations as the functioning day-to-day organs of allocation and distribution. Never having paid too much attention to the government anyway, the control associations performed about as well as they ever had; but the lack of supervision began to produce inflation and a leakage of products into the black market.

Because SCAP was initially most concerned with "democratizing" Japan, it ordered the Diet on December 20, 1945, to enact the National General Mobilization Law Abrogation Law, which eliminated the legal basis of the control associations. Thus the system of rationing and control became totally ad hoc for the first postwar year. As SCAP historians note, "Distribution functions continued to be administered by the presurrender control organizations whose dissolution had been postponed on a month-to-month basis pending the Government's assumption of these activities."[25]

During 1946, seeing the way things were going, several control associations followed the lead of the zaibatsu combines and declared their own dissolution. They then reconstituted themselves as "trade associations." For example, the Iron and Steel Control Association voluntarily abolished itself on January 8, 1946, an action SCAP approved a month later, but it soon reappeared as the Iron and Steel Council. These successor bodies were, as SCAP acknowledged, "con-

---

[25] SCAP, Monograph 34, "Price and Distribution Stabilization: Non-Food Program" (declassified May 25, 1971), *Historical Monographs,* p. 81.

trol associations in all but name."[26] As late as December 1950, SCAP was still trying to track down and liquidate control associations that had disguised themselves as trade associations.

On August 6, 1946, SCAP launched its first attempt to bring some order to Japan's disintegrating system of economic controls. In SCAPIN 1108, the Supreme Commander ordered the government to dissolve all *tōseikai* and to repeal or rescind all laws, ordinances, regulations, and ministerial notices relating to them. In place of this old system, SCAP required the government to create a new planning, allocation, and rationing agency, which the Japanese government duly supplied six days later in the form of the Economic Stabilization Board (ESB). This new board, according to SCAP's plan, was to establish public agencies under its control "to carry on the allocations of materials to and within specific industries selected by the ESB to assure production of essential materials and goods."[27] However, the ESB, under its first director-general, Zen Keinosuke, simply delegated authority to the old control associations, now reconstituted as trade associations, and nothing changed.

SCAP had failed to take account of two forces that were powerfully at work during this period: antimilitarism and bureaucratic rivalries. The old established ministries, such as Finance and MCI, were quietly but implacably opposed to a supraministerial body such as the ESB because it cut into their jurisdiction. They also had ammunition to oppose it: their contention that it was the same thing as the wartime, military-dominated Cabinet Planning Board, and, later, the General Mobilization Bureau of the Ministry of Munitions. This was accurate enough in terms of functions, although of course there was no military influence on the ESB. The ministries' goal was to brand ESB guilty by association, aided also by Prime Minister Yoshida's deep dislike of governmental economic planning of any sort. Things rested there until mid-1947, when SCAP again had to intervene.

Meanwhile, as economic conditions worsened (a situation in which the Communist party thrived), SCAP got around to enacting a replacement for the National General Mobilization Law. In addition to having been anemic from birth, the ESB still lacked a legal basis for its duties. At SCAP's urging, the Diet enacted the Temporary Demand and Supply Adjustment Law (Rinji Busshi Jukyū Chōsei Hō, law 22) on September 30, 1946, providing the government with ironclad economic control powers—the very powers Kishi had sought unsuccessfully in the late 1930s. Although SCAP intended the law to be temporary, it lasted until

---

[26] SCAP, "Elimination of Private Control Associations," p. 29.
[27] Ibid., p. 49.

the end of the occupation, and it gave the MCI and its successor, MITI, virtually unlimited authority to direct the economy. By the time the 1946 law was finally abolished, MITI had already acquired new control laws which allowed it to dominate Japanese economic policy until the beginnings of trade liberalization in the 1960s.

With its new law on the books but the economy still faltering, SCAP next turned to trying to make the ESB work. First, it issued SCAPIN 1394 of December 11, 1946, which "ordered the government to withdraw from industry the powers of distribution control, specifically the control over distribution of materials and products by the method of exclusive purchase and sale by a designated company or association."[28] To replace these industry controls, SCAP told the government "to submit plans for the conduct of distribution functions by public corporations."[29]

Second, on May 1, 1947, MacArthur personally ordered that all basic planning activities of the various ministries and agencies be concentrated in the Economic Stabilization Board. The ministries now recognized that they could no longer resist ceding their planning powers to the ESB, so they shifted to the time-honored device of taking over the ESB by sending to it Finance and Commerce and Industry officials on temporary detached service. The staff of the ESB jumped from 316 poorly qualified employees in 1946 to 2,000 elite bureaucrats in 1947.[30]

The stage was thus set to create the public corporations, which SCAP and the Japanese government called *kōdan*. Beginning in April and lasting through December 1947, the Diet enacted one law after another establishing some fifteen state corporations to replace the old *tōseikai*. Of these fifteen, eight were in the field of domestic distribution, four in foreign trade, two in industrial recovery, and one in price control. All were special legal entities, tax exempt, staffed by government employees, with all their fixed capital supplied by the government. They obtained working capital from loans from the Reconstruction Finance Bank. One such *kōdan* was the Coal Distribution Kōdan (Haitan Kōdan), created by law 56 of April 14, 1947. It replaced the Japan Coal Company, a national policy company of 1939, and performed the same functions as its predecessor: purchasing and selling all coal and coke at prices established by the Price Agency and the ESB. By 1949, the Coal Distribution Kōdan had 12,000 civil service employees. SCAP had not so much replaced the *tōseikai* as it had nationalized them.

---

28 Ibid., p. 57.
29 SCAP, "Price and Distribution Stabilization: Non-Food Program," p. 84.
30 Ōnishi Yukikazu, *Keizai kikaku-chō* [Economic Planning Agency] (Tokyo: Kyōiku Sha, 1975), p. 11.

Similarly, the Fertilizer Distribution Kōdan (Hiryō Haikyū Kōdan) bought all ammonium sulfate from the manufacturers and sold it to the agricultural cooperatives, which in turn distributed it to the farmers. The differential between the buying and selling price was covered by government subsidies from the Reconstruction Finance Bank (RFB)— the source of the so-called RFB inflation that SCAP and the Dodge Line brought under control during 1949. The Long Term Credit Bank notes laconically, "The Fertilizer Distribution Kōdan was a continuation of the same distribution system that existed during the war."[31]

The fifteen *kōdan* functioned as basic control organs between 1947 and 1951. The main difference between them and their wartime equivalents was that the *kōdan* were fully state-financed and state-operated public corporations, whereas the *tōseikai* were privately controlled cartels camouflaged by a veneer of governmental authorization. The significance of the *kōdan* lies in their relationship to the reshuffling of the Japanese power structure that took place during the occupation. Those who lost power, thanks to SCAP, were the military (completely) and the zaibatsu (partially). Those who gained power were the civilian economic bureaucrats. This is not an outcome necessarily to be deplored, particularly given the performance of the economic bureaucrats after the peace treaty, but it does have its ironic aspects. SCAP itself had not intended that the bureaucracy should enhance its powers while rival groups were losing theirs, and it made some (rather futile) efforts to reform the bureaucracy. Nevertheless, the results would have amused Tōjō, had he lived; and they certainly pleased Kishi, as he left Sugamo Prison and began his political comeback along a path that would lead to the prime ministership from 1957 to 1960.

---

[31] Nihon Chōki Shin'yō Ginkō, *Jūyō sangyō sengo nijūgo nenshi* [The history of important industries during the twenty-five postwar years] (Tokyo: Sangyō to Keizai, 1972), p. 272.

4
Financing

In every post office in Japan are posters saying, "The funds you deposit in the postal savings system are invested in public corporations and banks, starting with your own town or village, and they serve to make your town or village a better place to live."[1] Although only about 20 percent of these funds are invested directly in local governing bodies, there lies behind these posters a fascinating history and a complex set of institutions that played a critical role in Japan's postwar economic growth.

The annual scheme drawn up by the Ministry of Finance for spending postal savings and other trust funds deposited with the government is known as the Fiscal Investment and Loan Plan (FILP) (Zaisei Tōyūshi Keikaku), Japan's famous so-called second budget. (Actually it is the third separate, or unconsolidated, budget.)[2] Concerning the FILP, Sumida and Suzuki note, "Today it stands alongside the general account budget itself; the FILP is the basic prop of our annual fiscal policy."[3] And Isomura Eiichi contends, "The FILP is the key to the economic growth of our country." [4]

The FILP is a plan for loans and expenditures to be made from the government's various savings accounts and annuity programs. All

---

[1] Yasuhara Kazuo, Ōkurashō [Ministry of Finance] (Tokyo: Kyōiku Sha, 1974), p. 96.

[2] The three current budgets are the general account, the special accounts, and the FILP. During the Pacific War there were four budgets: the general account, the special accounts, the Ministry of the Imperial Household budget, and the special war accounts budget. The last remained open from its inception in 1937 until its dissolution in 1946.

[3] Sumida Satoru and Suzuki Hideo, Zaisei tōyūshi [Fiscal investment and loan funds] (Tokyo: Zaimu Shuppan K.K., 1957), introduction.

[4] Isomura Eiichi, ed., Gyōsei saishin mondai jiten [Dictionary of current administrative problems] (Tokyo: Teikoku Chihō Gyōsei Gakkai, 1972), p. 230.

such accounts are consolidated for planning purposes and combined with some direct appropriations and governmental borrowing from domestic and foreign sources to produce a single large account that is reserved for investments. Approximately 80 percent of such funds are lent directly to the special legal entities for their operations and capital investments, or are transferred to the special banks and *kōko*, where they are lent or expended according to the rules and policies of these corporations. The terms for the use of FILP funds are normally 6.5 percent interest for five to thirty years.

The FILP came into being in 1953, the first year after Japan regained its independence. Between 1953 and 1973, when law 7 of March 31, 1973, made it mandatory for the Ministry of Finance at least to show the plan to the Diet for approval, it was totally controlled by the economic bureacrats—formally, by the First and Second Fund Planning and Operations Sections, Financial Bureau (Rizai Kyoku), of the Ministry of Finance, and indirectly by the Industrial Finance Section, Industrial Policy Bureau (prior to 1973, the Enterprises Bureau), of MITI. In 1953 the FILP was 33.4 percent of the size of the general account budget and 4.5 percent of Japan's gross national product; twenty years later these figures had risen to 48.5 percent and 6.3 percent respectively (see tables 5 and 6).

All authorities agree that the idea of the FILP as it existed in 1953 and subsequent years was unprecedented in Japan; but that does not mean it had no history at all. Endō Shōkichi writes, "Today's meaning of fiscal investment and loan funds [*zaisei tōyūshi*] can be traced back only to the wartime period. . . . Postwar Japanese capitalism is the heir of the immediate prewar structure, although of course the domestic political and economic situation has changed fundamentally." [5] The officials of the Financial Bureau in charge of administering the FILP describe it simply as a "postwar technique." [6] In short, the systematic, planned use of government trust funds to finance public corporations dates only from 1953; but the funds themselves and various governmental uses (and misuses) of them go back to the Meiji period.

History of the Yokinbu

Two features of prewar Japanese finance are central to the origins of the FILP. One is individual saving in government institutions; the other is the existence of special banks charged with promoting economic

---

[5] Endō Shōkichi, *Zaisei tōyūshi* (Tokyo: Iwanami Shinsho No. 595, 1966), p. 69.
[6] Fukushima Ryōichi, Yamaguchi Mitsuhide, and Ishikawa Itaru, *Zaisei tōyūshi* (Tokyo: Ōkura Zaimu Kyōkai, 1973), p. 125.

Table 5
THE FILP COMPARED WITH THE GENERAL ACCOUNT BUDGET

Year	General Account Budget (100 million yen)	Annual Change (%)	FILP (100 million yen)	Annual Change (%)	FILP as % of G. A. Budget
1953	9,655		3,228		33.4
1954	9,996	3.5	2,820	−12.6	28.2
1955	9,915	−0.8	3,219	14.1	32.5
1956	10,349	4.4	3,497	8.6	33.8
1957	11,375	9.9	4,107	17.4	36.1
1958	13,121	15.3	4,174	1.6	31.8
1959	14,192	8.2	5,329	27.7	37.5
1960	15,697	10.6	6,069	13.9	38.7
1961	19,527	24.4	7,737	27.5	39.6
1962	24,268	24.3	9,052	17.0	37.3
1963	28,500	17.4	11,097	22.6	38.9
1964	32,554	14.2	13,402	20.8	41.2
1965	36,581	12.4	16,206	20.9	44.3
1966	43,143	17.9	20,273	25.1	47.0
1967	49,509	14.8	23,884	17.8	48.2
1968	58,185	17.5	26,990	13.0	46.4
1969	67,395	15.8	30,770	14.0	45.7
1970	79,497	18.0	35,799	16.3	45.0
1971	94,143	18.4	42,804	19.6	45.5
1972	114,676	21.8	56,350	31.6	49.1
1973	142,840	24.6	69,248	28.3	48.5

Note: Budget and FILP figures are for the original budget and for the initial plan and therefore do not show supplements or deficits.
Source: Fukushima Ryōichi, Yamaguchi Mitsuhide, and Ishikawa Itaru, Zaisei tōyūshi [Fiscal investment and loan funds] (Tokyo: Ōkura Zaimu Kyōkai, 1973), p. 67.

development. In May 1875, the Postal Bureau (Ekitei Kyoku) of the Ministry of Home Affairs created a system to enable citizens to deposit funds in savings accounts at post offices. The scheme was part of the government's campaign of direct economic development in progress at the time. In 1881, the Postal Bureau was transferred from the Home

Table 6
THE FILP COMPARED WITH GNP

Year	GNP (100 million yen)	FILP Amount (100 million yen)	FILP % Change over Previous Year	FILP as % of GNP
1953	75,264	3,374		4.5
1954	78,246	2,858	−15.3	3.7
1955	88,646	2,978	4.2	3.4
1956	99,509	3,268	9.7	3.3
1957	112,489	3,968	21.4	3.5
1958	117,850	4,252	7.2	3.6
1959	136,089	5,621	32.2	4.1
1960	162,070	6,251	11.2	3.9
1961	198,528	8,303	32.8	4.2
1962	216,595	9,513	14.6	4.4
1963	255,921	12,068	26.9	4.7
1964	296,619	14,305	18.5	4.8
1965	328,125	17,764	24.2	5.4
1966	384,495	20,854	17.4	5.4
1967	453,221	24,968	19.7	5.5
1968	533,680	27,833	11.5	5.2
1969	629,972	31,805	14.3	5.0
1970	732,481	37,987	19.4	5.2
1971	810,932	50,087	31.9	6.2
1972	952,248	60,455	20.7	6.3
1973	1,098,000	69,248	14.5	6.3

Note: Figures for GNP and FILP are actual amounts except for 1973, which shows estimate for GNP and planned expenditures for the FILP.
Source: Fukushima Ryōichi, Yamaguchi Mitsuhide, and Ishikawa Itaru, *Zaisei tōyūshi* [Fiscal investment and loan funds] (Tokyo: Ōkura Zaimu Kyōkai, 1973), p. 66.

Ministry to the newly created Ministry of Agriculture and Commerce (the MCI's predecessor). In 1885, the bureau itself became the Ministry of Communications (Teishin-shō), which went through numerous organizational changes until June 1, 1949, when it was abolished and replaced by the present Ministry of Posts and Telecommunications.

The old Postal Bureau called its savings service simply *yokin* ("deposits"), and when the system was regularized under the Teishin-shō, the ministry set up a Deposits Bureau (Yokin Kyoku) as part of its internal structure. The Deposits Bureau transferred the funds it collected at the post offices to the Ministry of Finance for safekeeping, and the Ministry of Finance labelled them *yokinbu*, meaning in this context "post office deposits account." The term *yokinbu*, like its successor *shikin un'yōbu* ("investment funds account"), in use since 1951, is merely the conventional name of a special account within the national treasury. Contrary to the usual implication of the word *bu*, and the mistranslations of many Japanese as well as foreign writers, these terms are not names of departments or units within the Ministry of Finance, which only briefly in the early Meiji period and in the late Taishō period had a Yokinbu and never had a Shikin Un'yōbu in the sense of a deposits department.

In May 1878, the National Debt Bureau (Kokusai Kyoku) of the Ministry of Finance began to draw on the accumulated postal savings as security for the national debt. This procedure was formalized in May 1885, when the Dajōkan (predecessor of the cabinet) enacted the Deposit Regulations (Yokin Kisoku), which entrusted the use of the postal savings exclusively to the minister of finance. Until the middle of the Meiji period, the postal savings were used only to secure the national debt, but in 1907 the minister of finance expanded the functions of the *yokinbu* account to include providing collateral for local bonds, Industrial Bank bonds, and Kangyō Bank bonds, and making loans to the general and special accounts.

The *yokinbu* funds grew enormously around the time of World War I, and this led to great temptation and eventually to scandal. Attempting to meddle in the confused mixture of warlord and revolutionary politics that existed in China in 1917 and 1918, Prime Minister Terauchi dispatched his personal secretary, Nishihara Kamezō, to see if he could bind various warlords to Japan through a series of loans. Nishihara managed to dispense about ¥295 million to Chinese warlords, most of it coming from the Yokohama Specie Bank, the Industrial Bank, Bank of Korea, and Bank of Taiwan, all government special banks. However, he failed to obtain any but the flimsiest of collateral for his loans, and the warlords defaulted on about 95 percent of the total. In China this instance of Japanese bribery of the country's ostensible rulers was one of the direct causes of the famous May Fourth Movement of 1919, a key event in the Chinese revolution. In Japan it had almost as serious consequences, as the minister of finance was forced to use the postal savings trust funds to bail out the government banks.[7]

The public outcry in Japan against the use of the citizens' savings to remedy Terauchi's blunders in China led to the first major reform of the system. In 1925, the Diet enacted the Ministry of Finance Yokinbu Special Account Law (law 25), which set very tight restrictions on the use of the trust funds and established a special nongovernmental council, the Yokinbu Funds Use Committee, to approve all disbursements. For the next few years the postal savings once again were used primarily for securing the national and local debt; but with the outbreak of war in the late 1930s, their use was broadened for a second time.

Except for the immediate post–World War II years, the *yokinbu* has expanded in size every year since the account was created. During the 1930s, small savers—workers, farmers, owners of medium and small businesses—put their extra income into the postal savings system, because they feared the possible insolvency of private banks after the panic of 1927 and because of patriotic appeals. (The interest rate on postal savings was not attractively high until quite recently.) As a percentage of all private bank deposits, the *yokinbu* grew from 14 percent in 1913 to 35 percent in 1933, and to 49 percent in 1943. (The postwar rates are 23 percent in 1953, 21 percent in 1963, and 23 percent in 1965.)[8]

With funds of this size in the treasury during a period of war preparation and actual war, the government naturally began to make grants and loans to the national policy companies, the control associations, and the munitions companies. Once again, most of these transactions were handled by the Industrial Bank and other special legal entities in the banking field. Yokinbu funds were invested first in Japan Steel, then in the war-related national policy companies, and particularly in the seven *eidan* (including the Tokyo subway) of the 1940s. In 1944, the government obtained still more trust funds from a system it had set up of old age, disability, and death insurance for workers (the *kōsei nenkin hoken*). The use of these trust funds partially to finance the war, combined with postwar inflation, greatly damaged the integrity of the governmental savings system in the eyes of the public. After the surrender, to try to preserve the people's savings and pensions, SCAP prohibited use of the various trust accounts for anything but loans to cooperatives and security for the debts of local governments.

---

[7] Ibid., pp. 127, 185; and John G. Roberts, *Mitsui* (Tokyo: Weatherhill, 1973), pp. 197-99.

[8] Endō, *Zaisei tōyūshi*, p. 23.

There the matter rested until 1949, when, under the Dodge Line, SCAP made the rapid economic rehabilitation of Japan its top priority.

The Industrial Bank and the RFB

Before we can explore the reform of the *yokinbu* system in 1951 and the additions to it of other accounts to form the FILP funds, we must go back and trace the development of the Industrial Bank of Japan and its postwar successors. For various reasons, including the economics of rapid development, the heritage of state domination, the tax system, and nationalistic opposition to the profit motive, Japan has always relied more on banks to raise industrial capital than on a market for the sale and trading of equity shares, even though it has accepted and made extensive use of the joint stock company.

During the occupation, SCAP did not understand this history very well and therefore was inclined to be suspicious of the banks' position. The American reformers were convinced that the prewar industrial finance banks were part of a munitions-makers' cabal. Besides, a capital market (being the American mode of supplying savings to industry) was thought to be superior to bank lending. The result of this attitude was that even when SCAP authorities and Japanese officials were trying to work together to rebuild the Japanese economy, they were always squabbling over these questions, and they often came to distrust each other's motives. Any talk of a governmental special bank by the Japanese was sure to arouse suspicions in SCAP that the Japanese were "relapsing," while the Japanese agreed privately that SCAP was infiltrated by New Deal zealots who neither understood capitalism nor trusted anything but American institutions.[9]

The major focus of this controversy was the nature and functions of the Industrial Bank of Japan (Nihon Kōgyō Ginkō) and its occupation successor as of 1947, the Reconstruction Finance Bank (RFB) (Fukkō Kin'yū Kinko). The Industrial Bank was based on a special law of March 1900, and it came into being two years later. Its purpose was to meet the strong demand for long-term industrial capital that accompanied the proliferation of joint stock companies around the time of the Russo-Japanese War. Backed by government guarantees, the bank generated capital by selling its own bonds at home and abroad;

[9] See, in particular, Watanabe Takeshi, *Senryōka no Nihon zaisei oboegaki* [Recollections of Japanese finance under the occupation] (Tokyo: Nihon Keizai Shimbunsha, 1966), pp. 300-30; Shioguchi Kiichi, *Kikigaki: Ikeda Hayato* [Verbatim notes: Ikeda Hayato] (Tokyo: Asahi Shimbunsha, 1975), p. 34; and Nihon Kaihatsu Ginkō, *Nihon kaihatsu ginkō 10 nenshi* [Ten-year history of the Japan Development Bank] (Tokyo: Nihon Kaihatsu Ginkō, 1963), p. 12.

and it played a major role in financing Japan's industrial expansion and its wars in the 1930s and 1940s. The bank's most important wartime function was providing short-term loans to munitions industries that had received war contracts. Such loans were guaranteed by the Bank of Japan—in other words, by the central government.

The Industrial Bank was owned by some 9,000 shareholders, although the bulk of the shares was held by the Imperial Household and a few big banks and trust companies.[10] In June 1948, in a memorandum on special banks, SCAP demanded that the old special banks be transformed into ordinary commercial banks or bond underwriting companies. For the next two years the Industrial Bank took the second route; then, in March 1950, it became an ordinary long-term credit bank for industry. But this did not mean that either the spirit or the personnel of the old Industrial Bank were removed from the scene.

More important than SCAP's attitude toward the Industrial Bank was its deep displeasure with the Reconstruction Finance Bank, which was not a wartime institution but a governmental special legal entity set up during the occupation. The idea for the RFB came primarily from two people. One was Ishibashi Tanzan, the well-known prewar editor of the *Oriental Economist* and minister of finance in the first Yoshida cabinet (May 1946 to May 1947), whom SCAP purged in 1947, not because of his wartime activities but because occupation officials did not like his economics. The other was Arisawa Hiromi, professor of economics at Tokyo University, adviser to the Economic Stabilization Board during the first Yoshida government, and inventor of the so-called priority production policy, which was Japan's first major economic rehabilitation and development scheme after the surrender.

Ishibashi's plan was to create an organ like the Industrial Bank which the government could use to finance Japan's economic recovery by frankly inducing inflation, forcing savings out of the people as they reduced consumption. Arisawa's contribution was his "theory of priorities" (*keisha no riron*). Put into policy terms, this theory called for government to designate certain key industries as the ones to lead the recovery: first of all coal, with steel, electric power, and fertilizer added soon afterwards. Government then would implement these priorities by providing (1) price subsidies to producers; (2) a rigorous allocation and rationing system using the *kōdan* and the Temporary Demand and Supply Adjustment Law; and (3) financing, with both investment and operating funds created by the RFB.

---

[10] Supreme Commander for the Allied Powers, Monograph 39, "Money and Banking," *Historical Monographs* (Washington, D.C.: National Archives, 1951), p. 5.

Everyone involved recognized that this plan entailed tremendous inflation and the miseries that would accompany it, and that it would produce, in SCAP financial adviser Joseph M. Dodge's famous phrase, a "rigged economy walking on stilts" (takeuma keizai), the two stilts being RFB-created money and American aid. Still, many Japanese leaders thought it was the best plan available (and, unlike most Americans, they argued in later years that it worked). One reason SCAP did not like the RFB was that it saw the bank as a Japanese reaction to SCAP's moves against the tōseikai: just as SCAP was ending the wartime munitions subsidies, the RFB was planning to start them up again, but under the rubric of "reconstruction" rather than "munitions." It is also worth observing, as Professor Maeda Yasuyuki does, that "the basis for these policies were Marxist theories inherited from the war, theories that emphasized thinking in terms of commodities rather than in terms of prices and markets." [11]

The Japanese government began in August 1946 by establishing the RFB, without SCAP's blessing, as a department (Fukkō Kin'yūbu) within the Industrial Bank. The following January the RFB came into its own as an independent special legal entity based on a special law (law 34 of October 7, 1946). Its first chairman was Itō Kenji, who had been president of the Industrial Bank since February 1946. Over him was the Reconstruction Finance Committee, chaired by Minister of Finance Ishibashi and including the director general of the Economic Stabilization Board, the minister of commerce and industry, the minister of agriculture and forestry, and the governor of the Bank of Japan.

Before April 1949, when SCAP adviser Dodge ordered the RFB to suspend operations, the bank issued bonds some eighty-four times. The bonds were worth a total of ¥168 billion, of which 69 percent was underwritten by the Bank of Japan; this was what was meant by "RFB inflation." The RFB's total disbursements were ¥132 billion. In fiscal year 1946, 53 percent of the RFB loans went for operating subsidies to private enterprises; in fiscal 1947, 51 percent; and in fiscal 1948, only 6 percent, since by this time the policy of pouring money into a few key industries was beginning to show results.[12]

One of the bank's prime inflation-producing activities was subsidizing the fifteen kōdan, which paid high prices to manufacturers for

---

[11] Maeda Yasuyuki, "Tsūshō sangyō seisaku no rekishi-teki tenkai" [The historical development of trade and industrial policy], Tsūsan jyānaru, May 25, 1975, p. 11.
[12] MITI, ed., Sangyō gōrika hakusho [The industrial rationalization white paper] (Tokyo: Nikkan Kōgyō Shimbunsha, 1957), p. 51. The Japanese fiscal year is from April 1 to March 31. Using calendar years, Endō records that during 1947, operating subsidies accounted for 56 percent of RFB loans, and during 1948 for 29 percent. Zaisei tōyūshi, pp. 86–87.

89

their products and charged low prices to the *kōdan*'s customers. As SCAP notes, "The government's special distribution corporations borrowed heavily from the RFB and in June 1947 the RFB became the sole organ for advancing funds to the *kōdan*." [13] The biggest industrial borrowers, however, were Japan Electric Power Generation and Transmission, Mitsui Mining, Mitsubishi Mining, Hokkaido Colliery, Kansai Electric Power, Ube Kōsan, Kantō Electric Power, Shōwa Denkō,[14] Meiji Mining, Tōshiba, and a few others. There is no doubt that these companies used their RFB funds to pay their workers and to buy a degree of labor peace in a period of great turmoil; but they also invested enough of the money to bring Japan's basic energy supply quickly back to prewar levels. The RFB was one of the principal causes of the inflation that made life in Japan so difficult during these years, but it also made lasting contributions to postwar Japanese government. As Endō Shōkichi observes, "This organ for supplying state capital to industry gave birth in our country to the idea that would grow into the FILP." [15]

By the time Joseph M. Dodge arrived in Japan in February 1949, inflation was only barely under control. In line with the new U.S. policy of getting Japan back on its feet economically and making it a secure ally in the Cold War, Dodge went to work to reform the government's fiscal policies. Among other things, he prohibited the RFB from issuing any more bonds; it spent the next three years recovering as much as it could of the loans it had already made and was dissolved and absorbed into the Development Bank on January 16, 1952.

Ikeda Hayato, finance minister in 1949 in the third Yoshida government, is rather proud of the RFB. By his calculation the RFB collected on all but 2.9 percent of its loans, though the Development Bank itself puts the RFB's recovery rate at only 25 percent on plant

---

[13] SCAP, "Money and Banking," pp. 36-37.

[14] The Shōwa Denkō Corporation made a unique contribution to damaging the reputation of the RFB in the biggest postwar corruption scandal before the Lockheed case. On June 23, 1948, Hinohara Setsuzō, president of Shōwa Denkō, was arrested and charged with corruptly receiving and misusing RFB funds. During the summer and autumn, Ninomiya Yoshimoto, vice-president of the Industrial Bank; Kurusu Takeo, director general of the Economic Stabilization Board in the Ashida government; and Ōno Bamboku, prominent conservative politician, were also arrested. On October 15, 1948, the Ashida cabinet was forced to resign because of the scandal, and in December former prime minister Ashida and sixty-three members of the Diet and senior bureaucrats were taken into custody and indicted. In October 1952 all were found guilty by the Tokyo District Court, but in February 1958, the Ashida group was found not guilty on appeal.

[15] Endō, *Zaisei tōyūshi*, pp. 82-83.

and equipment loans and 78 percent on operating subsidies.[16] In any case, Ikeda concludes, "It is not at all right to deny the significant role that the RFB played in the recovery of Japan's postwar economy. . . . Loans were effective to a considerable degree. It is fair to say that the RFB accomplished its purpose."[17]

Ishibashi and Ikeda believed in government funding of industries at any cost. SCAP, Dodge, and Ikeda's leading political opponent, Ichimada Naoto, governor of the Bank of Japan, opposed this view; they feared that inflation was driving Japan toward a Communist revolution, and that, in any case, inflation should be ended in order to create an exchange rate for the postwar yen and to restore foreign trade. In retrospect, it is only fair to add that the Americans and some Japanese lacked the vision to see the coming heavy and chemical industrialization of Japan. They still expected a light-industry, textile-based future for the country they governed. But the bureaucrats, politicians, and Marxist-trained professors who supported priority production during the occupation were attuned to both the failures of Japan's wartime economic performance and the need in the future to convert Japan from a light-industry, Asia-oriented economy to a heavy-industry, global-oriented economy. War-induced though it was, theirs was the more ambitious vision.

In addition to stopping the RFB's lending activities, Dodge also forced Ikeda to write a balanced budget (a practice Japan continued until 1966), and he created the Japanese-American exchange rate (US$1 = ¥360) that lasted until 1971. Dodge's deflationary policies produced a sharp recession, which was only overcome in the autumn of 1950 when Korean War orders from the U.S. armed forces began to flow in.

Dodge's new policies also caused a drastic reduction in and redirection of long-term capital funds. Money was no longer available for basic industrial investment (what investment there was from 1949 through 1950 shifted radically from coal and electric power to textiles and chemicals), and a real energy shortage began to develop in the

---

[16] Shioguchi, *Kikigaki: Ikeda Hayato*, p. 112. Compare *Nihon kaihatsu ginkō 10 nenshi*, p. 484. Also see Ikeda Hayato, *Kinkō zaisei, senryōka sannen no omoide* [Balanced fiscal policy: recollections of three years under the occupation] (Tokyo: Jitsugyō no Nihon Sha, 1952), passim.

[17] Ibid. Ikeda served as an official of the Ministry of Finance between 1925 and 1948. He was vice-minister of finance from February 1947 to March 1948. He then was appointed minister of finance from February 1949 to October 1952, and from December 1956 to July 1957. He also held the post of minister of international trade and industry from February 1950 to April 1950 (concurrently), from October 1952 to November 1952, and from June 1959 to July 1960. He ended his public career as prime minister from July 1960 to November 1964.

91

country. Throughout 1950, all the major industrial organizations petitioned Ikeda and Dodge (on his periodic visits to Japan) for relief. They argued that while they agreed inflation had to be stopped, the shutting off of RFB long-term loans was crippling industry. There was little money in private hands; SCAP's efforts to develop a securities market in postwar Japan were in their infancy (the Tokyo Stock Exchange, reformed by SCAP on the model of the San Francisco Stock Exchange, reopened only on May 14, 1949);[18] and the government seemed to be the only source of investment funds.

Counterpart Funds

There was, however, one other source that became very important during this period—U.S. aid. Until Dodge's first trip to Japan in the spring of 1949, the United States had supplied Japan with about $1.2 billion worth of commodities purchased in America with GARIOA (Government and Relief in Occupied Areas) and EROA (Economic Rehabilitation in Occupied Areas) funds appropriated by the U.S. Congress. The Japanese government then sold these commodities through its kōdan and deposited the yen proceeds in its Foreign Trade Fund Special Account. This grant aid amounted to about 70 percent of Japan's total dollar imports before 1949. The value of the aid could not be determined exactly because the Japanese government did not account for it separately. This irritated SCAP and Dodge, for they knew the Japanese government was using the aid to finance the RFB and to keep inflation from mounting so fast that the whole economy would collapse. Therefore, on April 1, 1949, with SCAPIN 1988, Dodge created the U.S. Aid Counterpart Fund to ensure that the U.S. government knew how its money was being spent.

What came to be called after this time "counterpart funds" (mikaeri shikin) were the yen proceeds from the sale in Japan of food, textiles, petroleum, and chemicals imported by SCAP and turned over to the Japanese government. These monies were deposited in the Counterpart Fund Special Account opened by the Ministry of Finance, and they could be spent only with SCAP's approval. This counterpart fund account was maintained until August 1953, when it was renamed the Industrial Investment Special Account, supplied with direct appropriations from the general account, and made a part of the FILP. The

---

18 Nihon Keizai Shimbun, Shōken-bu [Japan Economic Journal, Securities Department], ed., Kabuto-chō nijūnen [Twenty years of kabuto-chō] (Tokyo: Nikkei Shinsho No. 96, 1969), pp. 12-45. Kabuto-chō is the Wall Street of Tokyo. Also, SCAP, "Money and Banking," pp. 44-50.

total value of the counterpart aid and interest on it (as distinct from all aid received since September 1945) was, according to the Ministry of Finance, ¥334.3 billion, or about $929 million at ¥360 to the dollar.[19] During 1949, Dodge directed that the counterpart funds be used to assist the RFB in recovering its losses, but a year later this operation was virtually completed, and significant counterpart surpluses remained available for other uses.

The Export-Import Bank and the Development Bank

The years from 1950 to 1952 witnessed the forging of the institutions that would manage the high-speed growth economy of the 1950s and 1960s. During this period the Export-Import Bank and the Development Bank were created, and the *yokinbu* system was reformed. None of these innovations came easily, however. Ikeda and Dodge—following Ikeda's visit to America in April 1950 and Dodge's third trip to Japan in October 1950—had become reasonably close colleagues. (Morinaga Teiichirō, at the time chief of the secretariat of the Ministry of Finance and later vice-minister, recalls that a kind of student-teacher relationship developed between them, although one might ask with hindsight who was the student and who was the teacher.)[20] But General Courtney Whitney of SCAP's Government Section and other lesser SCAP officials balked at each of the Japanese government's reform proposals, and Ikeda regularly had to go over their heads to Dodge, who was himself only slowly brought around to support the Japanese approach to industrial finance. Ikeda also faced opposition from his rival Ichimada at the Bank of Japan, who genuinely doubted the wisdom of some of Ikeda's policies. Of course, Ichimada also saw political advantage for himself if they failed; in addition, he was trying to maintain his bank's territorial jurisdiction against inroads by Finance and MITI. Neither of the two new special banks nor the FILP attained their final form until after the occupation ended and Japan regained a free hand to do as it liked.

The breakthrough for Ikeda's policies came in the form of the Export Bank of Japan. SCAP was more amenable to this governmental proposal than to previous ones because its aim was to provide long-term credits to exporters of heavy industrial equipment, which meant the bank would contribute to Japan's earning more foreign exchange. Two contending drafts of the bank's charter circulated

---

[19] Fukushima et al., *Zaisei tōyūshi*, p. 220.
[20] Shioguchi, *Kikigaki: Ikeda Hayato*, p. 35.

throughout 1950. One called for a *kinko* with a strong private business orientation, staffed by civilians; the other suggested a *kōko* run by the government and staffed by active-duty bureaucrats. In the autumn of 1950, Dodge made his preferences known: he wanted still a third type—a bank, or *ginkō*, that would be even more independent of direct government controls than a *kinko* would. It should not compete with private banks; the government should supply all the capital; and the bank should not have the power to issue bonds or to borrow. On this basis the Export Bank of Japan Law was passed by the Diet in December 1950, and the bank opened its doors on February 1, 1951. It began operations with an authorized capital of ¥15 billion provided from the general account and from U.S. aid counterpart funds. Contrary to Dodge's idea of a civilian-dominated bank, however, the law specified that the prime minister should name the president of the bank and that the bank should be operated under the supervision of the Ministry of Finance. In April 1952, with the ending of SCAP's authority, the government revised the bank's charter to remove the other American restrictions and renamed it the Export-Import Bank of Japan.

Much more controversial was the Japanese government's proposal to create a development bank, intended to supply long-term loans for domestic economic reconstruction and industrial development. On October 2, 1950, the Banking Bureau of the Ministry of Finance wrote its first position paper on the subject. It called for the creation of an official organ that would provide long-term, low-interest industrial financing and that would stop the then prevalent use of short-term private bank loans for such purposes. It also proposed that the bank's capital be supplied from the government's trust funds, which had grown enormously during the postwar period of uncertainty. The ministry calculated that at the end of March 1950 (the end of the fiscal year) there was ¥198.6 billion in the *yokinbu* accounts, and it noted that every industrial organization in the land was calling on SCAP to lift its restrictions on their use.[21] To meet the needs of capital-starved industries, the Ministry of Finance suggested the creation of an Industrial Construction Finance Corporation (Sangyō Kensetsu Kin'yū Kōko), and it gave its draft proposal to Dodge when he arrived in Tokyo on October 7.

At a press conference on January 11, 1951, Ikeda elaborated on the ministry's proposed finance corporation, which he now called the Development Bank (Nihon Kaihatsu Ginkō). He said that the funds for the new special bank would come from the *yokinbu*, direct appropriations, counterpart funds, and recovered funds from the RFB. He also

---

[21] *Nihon kaihatsu ginkō 10 nenshi*, pp. 19-42.

contended that the new bank would differ from the Export Bank in that it would have the authority to issue bonds. However, when these ideas reached SCAP, the Americans reacted with horror. All SCAP's Government Section could see in the plan was a renamed RFB and a renewal of inflation. Given this hostility, Ikeda appealed directly to Dodge by letter on March 1, 1951; and on March 7, General William F. Marquat, head of SCAP's Economic and Scientific Section, relaxed his opposition.

Still, the compromise Dodge and SCAP arrived at was considerably different from what Minister of Finance Ikeda wanted. The new bank was not to be allowed to issue debentures, borrow funds, or grant loans to cover a borrower's operating expenses; its entire initial capital of ¥10 billion was to be provided from counterpart funds. The Japanese side had no choice but to accept these American conditions. On March 27, 1951, Ikeda introduced a bill in the Diet to create the Development Bank (law 108), and on March 31, the Diet passed it.

SCAP thought it had nipped in the bud any attempt to revive the RFB or the old Industrial Bank, but from these modest beginnings the Kaigin (Development Bank) rapidly expanded until it controlled the largest budget of any postwar special legal entity in the financial sector. The Kaigin opened for business on April 30, 1951, with a total staff of eighty employees, including forty-six managers, twenty-seven of whom were drawn from the Industrial Bank, the Kangyō Bank (also known as the Hypothec Bank), and the Bank of Japan. The Kaigin's first president was Kobayashi Ataru, the politically influential head of a life insurance company that had profited greatly from the war. He was personally chosen by Ikeda on the advice of Shirasu Jirō, Prime Minister Yoshida's right-hand man. Below him were Ōta Risaburō, formerly of the Bank of Japan and Ichimada's most trusted associate (which signified Ichimada's acquiescence in Ikeda's victory), and four directors: Nakamura Tateki, former Budget Bureau director of the Ministry of Finance (April 1945 to January 1946); Nakayama Sohei, a director of the Industrial Bank; Umeno Tomoo, chief of the Capital Funds Bureau of the Bank of Japan; and Yatabe Akira, chief of the Nihombashi Branch (Tokyo) of the Kangyō Bank.[22] All but Kobayashi were former bureaucrats, and all had been raised in the world of wartime finance and the Industrial Bank. They set out at once to enlarge their capital beyond the relatively small amount of counterpart funds SCAP had authorized.

---

[22] Abe Yasuji, *Ichimada Naoto den* [A biography of Ichimada Naoto] (Tokyo: Tōyō Shokan, 1955), p. 212; and Roberts, *Mitsui*, pp. 442-43.

Opening Up the Trust Funds

Meanwhile, the Ministry of Finance was working to loosen the restrictions on the *yokinbu* accounts. As early as October of 1950, Ikeda had proposed to Dodge a revision of the system then controlling the use of trust funds; and in December 1950, a change in the ministerial rules resulted in the first disbursements to public corporations such as the national railroads. By the time Dodge left Japan on December 5, 1950, he had approved Ikeda's plans to open up the trust funds completely to government use. On March 31, 1951, the Diet passed laws 100 and 101, which abolished the *yokinbu* accounts and replaced them with a single new special account called the *shikin un'yōbu* ("investment funds account"). This account for the first time combined postal savings, welfare pensions, national (social security) pensions, and other trust funds. The new laws also broadened the use of such funds to include loans to and collateral for the bonds of special legal entities.

To supervise expenditures from the *shikin un'yōbu,* the laws created a permanent deliberation council *(shingikai),* headed by the prime minister and with the ministers of finance and posts and telecommunications as vice-chairmen. The members of the *shingikai* included the vice-ministers (that is, the highest-ranking nonpolitical officials) of finance, welfare, the Economic Planning Agency (a post reserved for a high-ranking MITI official until 1969), and other agencies. Only five members were civilians. In 1961, the law covering the *shingikai* was revised and all members became civilians; since then the council has been composed primarily of financial experts who make recommendations on long-term loans and interest rates.

With the trust funds now once again available to the special legal entities, those that already existed began to draw on the new source of financing at once, and many new ones were set up to meet the country's pressing needs for electric power development, financing of medium and small enterprises, commercial aviation, and other companies and services. The *tokushu hōjin* that already existed were the Japanese National Railways (1949); the Bank for Commerce and Industrial Cooperatives (1936); the People's Finance Corporation (1949); and the Housing Loan Corporation (1950). New ones were the Nippon Telegraph and Telephone Public Corporation and the Electric Power Development Company, both created in 1952, and Japan Air Lines, the Smaller Business Finance Corporation, and the Agriculture, Forestry, and Fishery Finance Corporation, created in 1953. In addition, in July 1952, following the end of the occupation on April 28, the charter of the Development Bank was revised, giving the bank authority to issue its own bonds and lifting the ceiling on the size of the loans it could make.

96

Birth of the FILP

The surge in demand for funds, coupled with the proliferation of public corporations to spend or lend them, led to the creation of the Fiscal Investment and Loan Plan in 1953. The FILP had two purposes: to bring the disbursements of government capital under effective control, and to augment the *shikin un'yōbu* funds, which were large but not large enough. To set it up, several things were done. The old counterpart funds account was abolished and replaced by a new Industrial Investment Special Account, which was fed by direct appropriations and miscellaneous receipts from the American military forces. Funds held in trust from the post office life insurance system (separate from the postal savings system) were added to the plan. And receipts from government-guaranteed bonds and loans also contributed. The *shikin un'yōbu* was the prime source of funds for the FILP (see table 7), but the other sources were of great importance in the early years, particularly during recessions. It should be noted that the FILP was a creation of the Ministry of Finance and has been managed exclusively

Table 7
CONTRIBUTIONS TO THE FILP (1972 AND 1973)

Accounts	Amount (100 million yen) 1972	1973	Percent of FILP 1972	1973
Industrial investment special account	794	802	1.4	1.1
Shikin Un'yōbu funds	42,445	56,239	78.6	81.2
Postal savings	(17,000)	(23,000)	(31.5)	(33.2)
Welfare pensions	(12,106)	(14,480)	(22.4)	(20.9)
National pensions	(2,123)	(2,600)	(3.9)	(3.8)
Other	(11,216)	(16,159)	(20.8)	(23.3)
Post office life insurance	6,208	7,405	11.5	10.7
Bond and loan receipts	4,507	4,802	8.4	6.9
Totals	53,954	69,248	99.9[a]	99.9[a]

a Percentages do not add to 100 because of rounding.
Source: Calculated from Fukushima Ryōichi, Yamaguchi Mitsuhide, and Ishikawa Itaru, *Zaisei tōyūshi* [Fiscal investment and loan funds] (Tokyo: Ōkura Zaimu Kyōkai, 1973), p. 671.

by officials of that ministry's Financial Bureau to this day. The deliberation council set up in 1951 supervises only the *shikin un'yōbu*, not the FILP. Access to the Financial Bureau is thus a key source of power for other ministries and special legal entities, given Japan's bureaucratically dominated political process.

Only a year after establishing the FILP, its managers found themselves involved once again with the Americans. This came about because of the recession of 1954. Following the consumption boom of 1952, and the investment boom of 1953, a balance of payments squeeze developed in 1954. The general account budget declined by ¥27.7 billion from 1953, and Development Bank resources from the FILP dropped from ¥55.5 billion in 1953 to ¥33 billion in 1954. Under these circumstances the Japanese government turned to the program of surplus agricultural sales run by the U.S. Commodity Credit Corporation. In May 1955, the Japanese bought from the United States $85 million worth of surplus rice, wheat flour, skim milk, and other agricultural products—with 70 percent of the purchase price being lent to the Japanese by the Americans. In February 1956, another $65.8 million worth of surplus products changed hands. A third deal was broken off at the negotiation stage. The terms for repayment were forty years at 3 percent interest if repaid in dollars, or 4 percent if repaid in yen. The Japanese government sold the commodities domestically for yen, so the arrangement was similar to that for the counterpart funds from 1949 to 1953. The United States used part of the proceeds from the sales for American activities in Japan, such as maintaining the armed forces and sponsoring Fulbright scholars. The net gain for Japan was about ¥40 billion, which went to finance the Electric Power Development Company, the Aichi Prefecture Water Resources Corporation, and the Japan Productivity Center.[23]

During the period of high-speed growth, from 1953 to 1961, the government supplied between 38 percent (1953) and 21 percent (1961) of all capital invested in new industrial plants and equipment. Of government's share, its special financial entities (banks and *kōko*) contributed between 33 percent (1953) and 15 percent (1961); the rest came from special accounts. The Development Bank was by far the most important of the special legal entities, contributing 22 percent of all industrial investment in 1953 and 5 percent in 1961.[24] (The

---

[23] Endō, *Zaisei tōyūshi*, pp. 44-45; Fukushima et al., *Zaisei tōyūshi*, pp. 231-33; Sumida and Suzuki, *Zaisei tōyūshi*, pp. 763-74; and Tsūsan-shō Kisha Kurabu [MITI Journalists' Club], *Tsūsan-shō* (MITI) (Tokyo: Hōbunsha, 1958), pp. 101-15.

[24] Endō, *Zaisei tōyūshi*, p. 149.

reduction was due to the great expansion of private bank financing during these years.)

But the real importance of Kaigin loans came to be not their size but their role as indicators of the industries that government planners were prepared to support in many other ways. Firms that received a Development Bank loan had thereby received MITI's seal of approval (*osumitsuki*), and as businessmen say, "If the Kaigin has invested money, my city bank will lend me more."[25] Endō Shōkichi believes that the true significance of the FILP lies in its having made possible this guidance (*yūdō*) of private capital investment by the state.[26]

[25] Tsūsan-shō Kisha Kurabu, *Tsūsan-shō*, p. 24.
[26] Endō, *Zaisei tōyūshi*, pp. 174-75.

5
Control and Amakudari

The theory of the public corporation holds that a public activity can be carried on with full accountability and still achieve the effectiveness, efficiency, and political neutrality associated with private enterprise. To accomplish these things, the public corporation must be free of ministerial controls and parliamentary intrusions into its day-to-day operations, and it must be insulated from politics by its charter. The political community keeps the corporation accountable by requiring that it be audited like any other corporation and that its board of directors be held responsible for running the enterprise in a way that fulfills the terms of the corporate charter. Public enterprise thus differs from straight governmental bureaucracy in that it is judged partly by quantitative tests of the market, profitability, or financial performance.

It is precisely on these scores that Japanese analysts are most critical of Japan's public corporate sector. They note that the numerous special legal entities are subject to excessive supervision and control by the central government; that they commonly persist after their original purposes have been achieved; and that some of them are set up for the convenience of ministries or pressure groups, even if their functions are not appropriate to public corporations and should be performed directly by the state. The corporations are extensions of the official bureaucracy, it is contended, and yet they manage to avoid internal ministerial responsibility and they fail to demonstrate true corporate responsibility.[1] For example, the annual budgets and business plans of the *kōsha* and *kōko* are subject to a Diet vote, which is one reason for the exorbitant deficits of the Japanese National Railways, given

---

[1] Administrative Management Agency, *Government Corporations in Japan* (Tokyo: Administrative Management Agency, 1973), pp. 45-48; and Yoshitake Kiyohiko, *An Introduction to Public Enterprise in Japan* (Beverly Hills, Calif.: Sage Publications, 1973), pp. 131, 136.

politicians' reluctance to raise rates and thereby irritate voters. Likewise, the *kōdan* must receive the approval of their "competent minister" for their budgets and plans. All forms of special legal entity must receive ministerial authorization to issue bonds or to alter prices or rates (the Diet itself approves the prices and rates of the *kōsha* and *kōko*); even the road tolls of the highway construction *kōdan* are set by law. Generally speaking, Japan's public corporations have no monetary autonomy; their personnel have small scope for independent action; and their only freedom is in arranging their day-to-day operations. They are, in fact, extensions of the official bureaucracy, and they are best understood in that light.

By far the most notorious aspect of public corporate practice in Japan is the ministries' use of the corporations' boards of directors as retirement havens for their former bureaucrats. This custom, a subject of continuous concern and frequent exposés in the press, is part of what the Japanese public calls bureaucratic *amakudari* ("descent from heaven"). High-ranking career officials of the central government's ministries and agencies retire early by Western standards—almost invariably between the ages of forty-five and fifty-five—for reasons to be explained later. Upon retirement they obtain new employment of four different types. The first is in a private, profit-making enterprise, which is subject to minor legal restrictions. The second is in one of the 112 special legal entities. In virtual recognition of the fact that this form of reemployment is merely a shift to another branch of the government, it is commonly called "sideslip" (*yokosuberi*) rather than *amakudari*.

The third type of retirement is into politics: the bureaucrat stands for election to the Diet, most commonly as a candidate for the House of Councillors in the national constituency. This post-retirement career is sometimes called "position exploitation," referring to the fact that it is usually open only to bureaucrats who served in choice national or regional posts that are particularly advantageous for building general political support. Good posts from which to launch a political career include chief of the Forestry Agency or Food Agency in the Ministry of Agriculture and Forestry; chief of the Ports Bureau, Ministry of Construction; chief of the Medium and Small Enterprises Agency, MITI; chief of a regional bureau of MITI; chief of the Banking Bureau or National Tax Agency, Ministry of Finance; vice-minister of education; and chief of the Juvenile Homes Bureau, Ministry of Welfare.

The fourth form of retirement is into one of the several thousand auxiliary organs (*gaikaku dantai*), the type IV public policy companies identified in chapter 2. Reemployment in an auxiliary organ differs from

102

a post-retirement career in private business in that the various associations and foundations attached to a ministry are not profit-making organizations, so a position in one of them is not subject to the legal restrictions that apply to profit-making enterprises. Bureaucrats often spend a few years immediately following retirement as officials of auxiliary organs and then go on to make a true "descent" to a private business after the legal waiting period (which will be discussed in a moment) has expired. All ministries and agencies maintain a few auxiliary organs purely as *amakudari* landing spots for their hard-to-place retired officials. One analyst has charged that about 10 percent of all auxiliary organs are "sleeping legal entities" (*suimin hōjin*)—that is, foundations and associations with no other function than to pay salaries to retired bureaucrats.[2] An example is the Milk Transport Equipment Leasing Association, attached to the Ministry of Agriculture and Forestry and headed by a former director general of the Food Agency. Even though the Board of Audit found in 1969 that the association had engaged in no activities of any sort, the ministry in subsequent years still included several hundred million yen in its annual budget for the association's support.[3]

There are two kinds of legal restrictions on *amakudari*. The first covers bureaucrats' reemployment in a private, profit-making business. According to article 103 of the National Public Service Law (law 120 of 1947, amended by law 222 of 1948), "Personnel are hereby prohibited for a period of two years after leaving the public service from accepting or serving in a position with a profit-making enterprise which involves a close connection with any agency of the state . . . with which such persons were formerly employed within five years prior to separation from service." This law also establishes a National Personnel Authority which has among its various duties the power to grant exceptions to article 103 when it finds that no "close connection" exists between a retired official's former work and his proposed new employment.

After repeated protests from the press, public, and employees of firms receiving *amakudari* bureaucrats that the Personnel Authority was giving out exceptions too freely, the authority began in 1965 to

[2] Nagano Akira, *Kanryō* [Bureaucrats] (Tokyo: Seikai Kōron Sha, 1971), p. 128.
[3] Ino Kenji and Hokuto Man, *Amakudari kanryō* [Descended-from-heaven bureaucrats] (Tokyo: Nisshin Hōdō, 1972), p. 150. Still a fifth type of *amakudari*, one that is putting much greater central control over local government than was true at the end of the occupation, is bureaucrats descending into prefectural governments, often as vice-governors. On this aspect of descent from heaven, see Investigative Staff, " 'Amakudari kanryō tsuihō' sōdōki: Ibaraki-kensei" [Record of strife in the "purge of amakudari bureaucrats": the case of the Ibaraki prefectural government], *Kankai*, vol. 2, no. 8 (August 1976), pp. 100-106.

supply annual reports to the Diet on its activities for the previous year. The report, known to the press as the "Amakudari White Paper," lists and describes the bureaucrats at the level of section chief and above retiring each year, and explains the exceptions to article 103 it has granted. This reporting has not, however, stilled the public criticism of *amakudari*, since it shows that the authority's investigations consist largely of asking the minister of the organ from which an official has retired whether there is a close connection between the man's previous and proposed work. As we shall see, the minister has every incentive to deny that any connection exists.

The second legal restriction concerns bureaucrats' entry into politics. An amendment of May 10, 1962 (law 112) to the Election Law prohibits certain bureaucrats, including the vice-ministers of finance, agriculture, and construction, from entering the first House of Councillors election called after their retirement.[4] But neither this restriction nor article 103 has done much more than slow down the process of *amakudari*. At best, the restrictions merely divert a certain number of retired officials into a special legal entity or an auxiliary organ for a few years before they move on to something more attractive. (Of course, some of them never do move on.)

Despite its prevalence, *amakudari* is not uniformly popular with retired officials. The most famous instance of a senior bureaucrat's refusing to take a post-retirement executive position (instead he became for a time a *rōnin*, or masterless samurai) was Sahashi Shigeru, vice-minister of MITI from October 23, 1964 to April 25, 1966. Sahashi gives three reasons for his virtually unprecedented action:

> First, if you descend to a private firm, all you do is to block the promotions of internal employees who would like to advance to the position you occupy. This is a very unpleasant situation in which to try to work. Second, if you go into a government corporation, even if you become its president, you still have to bow your head to the current vice-minister of the supervising ministry. This is not a role that suits me. Third, if you become a Diet member, you must do the bidding of your financial backers. There's nothing to do in the Diet until the election system is changed.[5]

---

4 Shibuzawa Kijirō, *Kōkyū kōmuin no yukue, minkan amakudari to rikkōhō seigen mondai* [Tracking down higher civil officials: the problems of descent from heaven to civilian life and the qualifications of election candidates] (Tokyo: Asahi Shimbun Chōsa Kenkyū Shitsu, Internal Report no. 120, May 10, 1966), pp. 8-9.

5 Kusayanagi Daizō, "Sahashi Shigeru, amakudaranu kōkyū kanyrō" [Sahashi Shigeru, a senior bereaucrat who did not descend from heaven], *Bungei shunjū*, May 1969, p. 174.

Even so, after holding out for a few years, Sahashi became chairman of the board of the Leisure Development Center (Yoka Kaihatsu Sentā), one of MITI's numerous auxiliary organs.

When I spoke with Sahashi in Tokyo in 1974, he commented that in the cases of retiring bureaucrats who are not wanted by private businesses, because they lack talent or are too bureaucratic, their ministries must place them in public corporations, where the government has complete control over personnel matters.[6] This remark is typical of the man who was MITI's most illustrious—and certainly its most outspoken—postwar vice-minister; but it also suggests that there is a definite hierarchy of prestige among the various *amakudari* routes. MITI officials much prefer—and dominate—descent into big business, while Finance officers tend to go primarily to the public corporations. Agriculture, and also Finance, lead in sending ex-bureaucrats into politics, while Education and Foreign Affairs are forced by lack of connections to rely primarily on their own auxiliary organs.

Normally the job of placing the annual crop of retirees falls to a sitting vice-minister or chief of secretariat. In general, he tries first for straight *amakudari* into business. Some of those who fail to qualify there will be placed by the leaders of their ministry in the public corporations the ministry controls. In a really tight year, the ministry may even try to set up a new corporation or split an old one into two new ones. Those bureaucrats who enter politics are in a special category, since they will have obtained political support, financing, and a patron in the Liberal Democratic Party. The few retirees who are left will end up in the auxiliary organs.

Why Amakudari?

Why do Japan's higher officials—holders of what are indisputably the most prestigious positions in the Japanese social system—retire so early? And having done so, why do they have to find new employment? The answers to these questions are complex, for the Japanese system of retirement and reemployment is a product of the country's whole history and is part of the norms of official bureaucratic life in Japan.[7] In

---

6 Interview with Sahashi Shigeru, September 5, 1974.

7 See, for example, Chalmers Johnson, "The Reemployment of Retired Government Bureaucrats in Japanese Big Business," *Asian Survey*, vol. 14, no. 11 (November 1974), pp. 953-65. The most important general works in English on the bureaucracy are Robert M. Spaulding, Jr., *Imperial Japan's Higher Civil Service Examinations* (Princeton: Princeton University Press, 1967); and Kubota Akira, *Higher Civil Servants in Postwar Japan* (Princeton: Princeton University Press, 1969).

essence, the officials must retire because of the rigid age-grading and seniority system that prevails throughout the bureaucracy, and they must find new employment because retirement benefits are inadequate for a man who finds himself out of work at fifty. The retirement system is also a product of the intrabureaucratic competition over jurisdiction that affects all ministries; it also promotes the Japanese organizational value of frictionless decision making by maintaining a bureaucratic old-boy network throughout the society.[8]

Perhaps the most immediate reason for Japanese bureaucrats' early retirement is the enormous number of people in the bureaucracy. Bureaucrats in prewar and wartime Japan fell into three categories: *chokunin, sōnin,* and *hannin.* Between 1932 and 1946, the numbers of *chokunin* ("by Imperial appointment") and *sōnin* ("appointed with Imperial approval") officials grew from 13,400 to 29,543. The total number of central government bureaucrats (including *hannin* officers, appointed at the discretion of the competent minister) rose from 109,888 to 256,218.[9] In 1948, these three general ranks were reclassified as first-, second-, and third-class officers. The trend since then has been toward further expansion. Whereas between 1894 and 1943, some 9,008 persons passed the Higher Civil Officials Examination, from 1948 to 1973 the number of passers was 18,998.[10] This growth of the bureaucracy placed intense strains on its strict seniority system.

Ever since the late Meiji period, all bureaucrats have entered the government service immediately following graduation from Tokyo University (and a few other universities that try feebly to compete with Tōdai in supplying bureaucrats). Thereafter they are promoted regularly, and transferred among sections of a ministry, according to the number of years served by the whole entering class. However, promotion and transfer are automatic only up to the section chief level. After that, increasingly fewer members of each class can hope to advance to a key executive position—chief of the General Affairs Section of a bureau or an agency, chief of one of the three sections in a ministry's secretariat, deputy bureau chief, chief of a home office

---

[8] See Ezra F. Vogel, ed., *Modern Japanese Organization and Decision-making* (Berkeley and Los Angeles: University of California Press, 1975).

[9] Supreme Commander for the Allied Powers, Monograph 13, "Reorganization of Civil Service," *Historical Monographs* (Washington, D.C.: National Archives, 1951), microfilm frames 586-87.

[10] Watanabe Yasuo, "Kōmuin no kyaria" [Careers of public officials], in Tsuji Kiyoaki, ed., *Gyōseigaku kōza* [Lectures on the science of public administration] (Tokyo: Tokyo Daigaku Shuppankai, 1976), vol. 4, pp. 179-81. The difference between the total numbers of *chokunin* and *sōnin* officers and the examination passers is explained by the fact that not all prewar officials took the exams, and some were military officers.

bureau, director general of an "external bureau" (*chō*, or agency), or administrative vice-minister (*jimu-jikan*), the highest nonpolitical officer in a ministry. As members of a particular entering class are selected for these positions, those of the same class who do not make it are obliged by precedent to resign. That is, when a member of a class becomes vice-minister, all other officials in his ministry from the same class must resign, leaving the vice-minister with absolute seniority.

These general rules pertain in all ministries, although with some slight differences in detail. The Ministry of Construction, for example, allows technical officers to advance to the vice-ministership in rotation with administrative officers. There is also some difference in the length of service each ministry requires before the weeding out begins. As of December 1, 1975, for example, the Ministry of Finance's class of 1958 was just receiving its first section chief appointments; the three secretariat section chiefs were from the classes of 1951 and 1952, the internal bureau chiefs from 1946 to 1948, the external bureau chiefs from 1946, and the vice-minister from the class of 1944. At MITI, the class of 1961 was moving into the section chiefs' offices and the class of 1944 held the vice-ministership; at Agriculture the parallel classes were 1960 and 1943, at Transportation 1961 and 1943, and at Construction 1958 and 1944.

The prewar and wartime expansion, by creating more low-level posts, so clogged the system with candidates for the higher posts that the postwar promotion rate has been stretched out by about ten years. For example, Kaya Okinori entered the Ministry of Finance in the class of 1917 and became vice-minister in 1937, an elapsed time of twenty years, while Takeuchi Michio entered in 1944 and became vice-minister in 1975, an elapsed time of thirty-one years. Similarly, Kishi Nobusuke entered the Ministry of Commerce and Industry in 1920 and became vice-minister in 1939, an elapsed time of nineteen years, while Komatsu Yūgorō, class of 1944 and vice-minister in 1974, took thirty years to do the same. All top officials are under great pressure to retire by at least the age of fifty-five in order not to lengthen the waiting period for their juniors any more.

Early forced retirement for those officials who do not proceed beyond the section chief level developed as a way of keeping the size and age of the bureaucracy under control. Even those officers who become bureau chiefs and above remain in those posts for only a few years—until they are pushed out by the classes advancing inexorably from below. If a vice-minister should remain in his position much longer than about two years, the members of the classes below him become extremely concerned that their year will be skipped and that no one from their cohort will make it to the top post. For a vice-minister to hold his office for, say, five years, he must maneuver to eliminate from the service (and find good *amakudari* landing spots for) all the talented figures in the classes immediately junior to his—a practice that is not at all uncommon. Obviously, this custom fuels the factional infighting that goes on in all important ministries.[11]

Good post-retirement employment makes the system tolerable; it is said to cause bureaucrats to "grow young again." Such employment is also a financial necessity, both because of the government's comparatively meager retirement benefits and as compensation for the years of prestigious but low-paying service as a *kōkyū kōmuin* ("higher civil servant"). For example, the monthly salary of a vice-minister in 1969 was ￥260,000 ($722.22 at ￥360=US$1); by comparison, a minister's monthly salary was about ￥430,000, and the governor of Tokyo made about ￥300,000 per month. As we shall see, even these salaries were less than that of the president of a public corporation.

Upon retirement, a vice-minister is compensated in two ways. First, he receives a substantial lump sum which is calculated according to a complex formula. The size of this sum is legally limited to 60 times his monthly salary, but the average is usually about half that. Yoshitake Kiyohiko says that a vice-minister after twenty-five years of service would receive about ￥10,732,800; my own independent computation produces a figure of ￥8,775,000 ($24,375), or 33.75 times the monthly salary.[12] In addition, beginning at age fifty-five and continuing until his death, a vice-minister receives a pension of 40 percent of his annual salary plus 1.5 percent for every year served beyond twenty years, up to an absolute limit of 70 percent. To be eligible for this pension, he must have been a member of, and contributed to, his ministry's mutual aid association for more than twenty years. The government contributes 55 percent of an official's annuity (National Public Service Mutual Aid Association Law, law 69 of June 30, 1948). On this basis, a vice-minister with twenty-five years of service would receive ￥123,500 ($343.05) per month.

These sums are not slight, but their purchasing power is less than the equivalent benefits prewar officials received; and they are consider-

---

[11] For a good summary of the state of the factional struggle within MITI in 1975, see Nawa Tarō, "Kankai jinmyaku chiri" [Geography of personal relationships within the bureaucratic world], *Kankai*, vol. 1, no. 1 (November 1975), pp. 80-88.

[12] Yoshitake, *Public Enterprise in Japan*, p. 237. For the salaries and formulas, see Ino and Hokuto, *Amakudari kanryō*, p. 99; and Shibuzawa, *Kōkyū kōmuin no yukue*, pp. 22-23.

ably less than a talented man could earn in private industry. More important than their absolute size is when they begin. A government official retiring at fifty will not even begin to receive his pension for five years (that is, at age fifty-five), and when it starts he will suffer a 50 to 60 percent cut in pay—all this coming just when his children are entering the university. Fortunately for him, however, these problems need not arise. By moving into the *amakudari* system on retirement, most high-ranking officials greatly strengthen their financial positions—so much so that some critics of the bureaucracy contend that official service has become nothing more than an apprenticeship for the big payoff years of retirement.[13]

Descent into Business

The best salaries to be made after retirement are in big business, and it is access to those private companies' boards of directors that makes a MITI career one of the most attractive to ambitious bureaucrats. In 1974, the president of New Japan Steel, the nation's largest profit-making enterprise, was Hirai Tomisaburō, MITI vice-minister between 1953 and 1955; the president of Tōshiba was Tamaki Keizō, MITI vice-minister between 1952 and 1953; the executive director of the Tokyo Electric Power Company, the world's largest privately held utility, was Ishihara Takeo, MITI vice-minister between 1955 and 1957; the executive director of the Toyota Motor Company was Yamamoto Shigenobu, MITI vice-minister between 1966 and 1968; and the vice-president of Arabian Oil was Ōjimi Yoshihisa, MITI vice-minister between 1969 and 1971.

For those bureaucrats who do not make the right connections in big business while in office, a move to the governmental corporations is almost as profitable—and public corporations offer one or two unusually lucrative features, as we shall see, that are not normally available in private enterprise. Even an occasional MITI vice-minister takes this route, as did Morozumi Yoshihiko (vice-minister between 1971 and 1973) when he became president in 1975 of the Electric Power Development Company, a *tokushu kaisha* set up in 1952.

In 1969, the monthly salary of the president of the Electric Power Development Company was ¥470,000, or about ¥40,000 more than that of a cabinet minister. The presidents of some fourteen other special legal entities, including the Export-Import Bank, the Develop-

---

[13] See, for example, Misonō Hitoshi, "Keizai kanryō no kinō to kongo no hōkō" [The functions of the economic bureaucracy and its future course], *Keizai hyōron*, vol. 17, no. 2 (February 1968), p. 13.

ment Bank, and the Bank for Commerce and Industrial Cooperatives, earned the same amount. Salaries for such top posts rise at a rate of about ¥30,000 to ¥40,000 each year, and in 1969 they stood at some ¥140,000 over the level of 1962–1963. But even more important than the salaries are the retirement benefits the special legal entities provide. A member of the board of directors of a government corporation receives on retirement a lump sum consisting of 65 percent of his monthly salary for each month he was employed. Since a president or chairman of the board of a special legal entity serves by law for a fixed term (three or four years), an individual bureaucrat can go from one special legal entity to another, receiving a huge retirement payment every time. Ex-bureaucrat executives who move from one government corporation to another are known as *wataridori* ("migratory birds").[14]

For example, a president of a *kōdan* or a *kōko* who served two terms (eight years) and retired in 1969 would have received on retirement the incredible sum of ¥29,328,000—$81,467 at the prevailing exchange rate. By contrast, an ordinary employee who worked for the same *kōdan* or *kōko* for 36 years could receive a maximum of only ¥5,670,000.[15] This discrepancy was, of course, created by the ministerial bureaucrats who wrote the laws setting up the corporations, and they did so with the intention clearly in mind of compensating themselves and their fellow officials for their low active-duty salaries. Retirement allowances for executives of the public corporations average two or three times what those same men received when they retired from the regular government service—and they are paid after only three or four years whereas the normal benefits must be earned by twenty to twenty-five years of service.

When Suzuki Keiichi retired after twelve years (May 1950 to May 1962) as president of the Housing Loan Corporation (a *kōko*), he received a retirement payment of around ¥2 billion.[16] He was, however, a stationary bird. One well-known "migratory bird" is Funayama Masakichi, who worked at the Ministry of Finance from 1928 to 1953 and was vice-minister of finance from April 20, 1951 to August 14, 1953. Upon retirement he was offered and took up, one after the other, the positions of director of the Bank of Japan, vice-president of the Japan Monopoly Corporation, vice-president of the Export-Import

[14] Yamamoto Masao, ed., *Keizai kanryō no jittai* [The reality of the economic bureaucracy] (Tokyo: Mainichi Shimbunsha, 1972), pp. 192-95, and Ino and Hokuto, *Amakudari kanryō*, pp. 20-24.

[15] Ino and Hokuto, *Amakudari kanryō*, pp. 98-103.

[16] Ibid., p. 100; and Kensetsu-shō Nijū-nenshi Henshū Iinkai, *Kensetsu-shō nijū-nenshi* [Twenty-year history of the Ministry of Construction] (Tokyo: Kensetsu Kōhō Kyōgikai, 1968), p. 417.

Bank, president of the Smaller Business Finance Corporation, and director of Japan National Railways. He was paid a retirement bonus every time he left one position and accepted another. Similarly, Kōno Tsūichi, class of 1932 at Finance and chief of the Financial Bureau when he retired on June 11, 1957, worked after "retirement" as a director of the Development Bank, deputy chairman of the board of the Bank for Commerce and Industrial Cooperatives, president of the People's Finance Corporation, and vice-president of the Bank of Japan. Needless to say, his experience as chief of the bureau that creates and controls each year's Fiscal Investment and Loan Plan was invaluable to these corporations, which are funded from the Plan.

An additional reason for these patterns of migration, other than improved retirement benefits, is to open up the lower slots for new retirees. The table at the end of this chapter lists the chief executive officers and their backgrounds as of 1975 for each of the fifteen *kōdan*, which are the heart of the public corporate sector. It will be seen that all but one of these men are former central government bureaucrats (the exception came from the Osaka municipal administration), and several are migratory birds.

Controlling the Landing Spots

Every analyst of Japanese government corporations explains their explosive growth in the postwar world as due in part to the needs of the ministries to create and control *amakudari* landing spots.[17] According to a study made by the Administrative Management Agency in 1967, the 112 special legal entities existing at that time had a combined total of 757 directors and higher executives. Of these 398 (52.6 percent) were ex-bureaucrats. When the total number of special legal entities is limited to the important ones with large budgets (the *kōdan*, *jigyōdan*, and *kōko*), the executive positions available number 276, with 210 (76 percent) held by former high-ranking officials. The leading sources of these *amakudari* bureaucrats were Finance, 39; Agriculture, 38; Construction, 28; and MITI, 26.[18]

The big growth years for special legal entities were 1962 and 1963, during the Ikeda administration, when a total of twenty-four new ones were created (see table 4 in chapter 2). During those years, an ava-

---

[17] In addition to the works already cited, see Sahashi Shigeru, "Kanryō shokun ni chokugen suru" [Straight talk to the gentlemen of the bureaucracy], *Bungei shunjū*, July 1971, p. 115; and "Amakudari no 'ronri'" [The "logic" of descent from heaven], *Sandē mainichi*, April 14, 1974, pp. 28-30.

[18] Misonō, *Keizai hyōron*, p. 14.

lanche of retirees from the war expansion classes of 1937 to 1942 came up for *amakudari*; and the chief secretary in every ministry was doing everything he could to expand his outlets for deserving officials. One authority calculates that in 1963 alone, a total of 721 retired section chiefs and above had to be placed.[19]

In addition to creating new special legal entities, some ministries divided old ones. For example, the Ministry of Construction had set up the Japan Highway Public Corporation in 1956. In 1959, the ministry spun off from it a new *kōdan*, the Tokyo Expressway Public Corporation; and in 1962 it spun off another *kōdan*, the Hanshin Superhighway Corporation. This action gave Construction three boards of directors to fill with retirees instead of one. Similarly, in 1964 the Ministry of Transportation created the Japan Railway Construction Corporation as a separate *kōdan* with an independent board of directors, even though the work it does had formerly been under the Japan National Railways, which Transportation also controls. There are other examples of this kind of fission, all of them influenced by *amakudari* considerations.[20]

Given the ministries' use of the public corporations to provide well-paid (and in the minds of most former officials, well-deserved) executive positions, informal norms have developed governing the assignment of available positions in a single corporation to various ministries. Sometimes these allocations are negotiated by the sponsoring ministry and the Budget Bureau of the Ministry of Finance when the proposal to set up a new corporation comes under budgetary review. For example, out of eleven executive posts in the Housing Loan Corporation (president, vice-president, seven directors, and two auditors), six are reserved for *amakudari* bureaucrats: the Ministry of Construction controls the presidency, Finance names the vice-president, Construction supplies two directors, and the Prime Minister's Office and the Economic Planning Agency are allowed to send one director each. The Japan External Trade Organization (JETRO), under MITI's control, reserves five of its nine executive posts for bureaucrats descended from heaven: MITI sends two, Foreign Affairs one, Agriculture one, and one is open to negotiation between MITI and another ministry. Some corporate boards are entirely used for *amakudari*. Agriculture's Hachirōgata New Community Development Corporation divides its five executive slots into three for Agriculture, one for Home Affairs, and one for another ministry in need; and MITI's Coal Mine Damage

---

[19] Shibuzawa, *Kōkyū kōmuin no yukue*, p. 16.

[20] Fukushima Ryōichi, Yamaguchi Mitsuhide, and Ishikawa Itaru, *Zaisei tōyūshi* (Tokyo: Ōkura Zaimu Kyōkai, 1973), p. 257.

Corporation allocates its seven executive posts to MITI (six) and Agriculture (one). These assignments are, of course, well known to vice-ministers and chief secretaries as they plan their annual job allocations for their classmates and juniors. The leaders of a ministry exert maximum pressure when a new corporation is being set up to ensure that their ministry gets a spot or two, depending on the ministry's relations with the sponsoring ministry and on the jurisdiction in which the new corporation is intended to operate. From the point of view of the corporation, a mix of ex-bureaucrats on the board of directors is useful for getting the organization's work done smoothly. Thus, for example, the Japan Highway Public Corporation reserves seven of its twelve directorships, including its presidency, for its controlling ministry, Construction. But since it needs financial support from the Ministry of Finance, it also takes a director from that ministry; and since highways are part of the transportation system, it recognizes the Ministry of Transportation's claim to one directorship. The corporation also finds it useful to give one director's slot to the Ministry of Home Affairs (even though it is not a very powerful ministry), to ensure its help in land requisition problems and relations with local governments. Before any particular public corporate structure is set, a lot of time must be spent in interministerial negotiation; but after that it works smoothly and is rarely changed.

The official explanation for the existence of bureaucratic *amakudari* is that it helps solve the problems of a civil service that is large and poorly paid in comparison to its responsibilities. In addition, true to the Japanese ability to make a virtue out of necessity, the *amakudari* system has developed other, more important (although less often acknowledged) functions. These are, above all, maintaining coordination and cooperative interaction among the state, the public corporate sector, and the private sector—an aspect of what the Japanese call *nemawashi* (literally, "preparing the groundwork") and what foreigners describe variously as consensual decision making or as an interlocking directorate among the bureaucracy, the conservative party, and the business community. Cyril Black and his associates write, "One of the best indicators of elite homogeneity in . . . Japan is the frequency of 'elite interpenetration' by which members of one segment of the administrative leadership transfer to another with little difficulty, thereby creating overlaps that further enhance the system's ability to respond to conflicts of interest." [21]

---

[21] Cyril E. Black et al., *The Modernization of Japan and Russia* (New York: Free Press, 1975), p. 269.

Many foreign observers of Japan have ascribed Japan's unusual gift for cooperation and avoidance of conflict in an advanced industrial society to Japanese national character. As this discussion shows, however, this Japanese talent is not merely a social given; it grows out of carefully nurtured and controlled institutions such as "descent from heaven" for retired officials.[22]

Bureaucratic leaders occasionally have acknowledged that they use *amakudari* to serve policy purposes. In 1940, vice-minister Kishi and General Affairs Bureau chief Shiina of the Ministry of Commerce and Industry did not disguise the fact that they sent Ōwada Teiji, the retiring vice-minister of Communications, to take over the presidency of the Nippon Soda Company because the then president, Nakano Yūrei, had displeased the military and the reform bureaucrats by not moving fast enough to integrate his chemical firm with the war effort.[23] Similarly, in 1971, MITI placed one of its former vice-ministers, Kumagai Yoshifumi, on the board of Sumitomo Metals after a bitter dispute with that company in 1965, when it had refused to follow MITI's "administrative guidance." In much less dramatic cases, assigning active-duty officials to work for short periods in the government corporations, and placing retired senior bureaucrats on their boards of directors, ensures that the government's views will be heard, while the public corporate form also affords a measure of independence and private expertise that is lost in completely state-operated enterprises.

---

[22] For another sector in which Japan's exceptionally good performance by international standards is better explained by its institutions than by its "national character," see David H. Bayley, *Forces of Order, Police Behavior in Japan and the United States* (Berkeley and Los Angeles: University of California Press, 1976).

[23] Miki Yōnosuke, *Keizai jiken no shuyaku-tachi* [Leading personalities of the economic scandals] (Tokyo: Sankei Shimbunsha, 1968), pp. 95-106.

Table 8
THE CHIEF EXECUTIVE OFFICERS OF THE FIFTEEN KŌDAN
March 1975

1. **Water Resources Development Public Corporation** (four-year term)
President Yamamoto Saburō
Yamamoto was an official of the Home Ministry and the Ministry of Construction from 1933 to 1963. He was vice-minister of Construction from November 1, 1961 to July 23, 1963. Between 1963 and 1974 he was an official of Mitsui Real Estate. He became president of the *kōdan* in May 1974.

2. **Regional Promotion and Facilities Corporation** (four-year term)
President Hirata Keiichirō
Hirata served as an official in the Ministry of Finance from 1931 to 1957. He was vice-minister of Finance from July 19, 1955 to May 31, 1957. Upon retirement he served as a vice-president of the Development Bank, and he was president of the *kōdan* from October 1972 to September 1976.

3. **Forest Development Corporation** (three-year term)
Chairman of the Board Matsuoka Makoto
Matsuoka was an official of the Ministry of Agriculture and Forestry from 1939 to 1965. He retired as director general of the Fisheries Agency. After retirement he served successively as head of the Hachirōgata New Community Development Corporation, Japan Sugar Price Stabilization Agency, and the Forest Development Corporation (October 1972 to September 1975).

4. **Agricultural Land Development Corporation** (three-year term)
Chairman of the Board Ōwada Keiki
After serving in the Ministry of Agriculture and Forestry from 1942 to 1961 and retiring as head of the Fisheries Agency, Ōwada worked in the Agriculture Ministry's auxiliary organs until June 1974, when he moved to the *kōdan*.

5. **Japan Petroleum Development Corporation** (three-year term)
President Shimada Yoshito
Shimada served in MITI from 1939 to 1966, heading the Enterprises Bureau from June 23, 1963 to April 25, 1966. He moved on retirement to the *kōdan*, which was set up in 1967.

6. **Internal Passenger Ship Corporation** (four-year term)
Chairman of the Board Kameyama Noburō
An official of the old Ministry of Communications (Teishin-shō) and the Ministry of Transportation from 1941 to 1968, Kameyama retired as director general of the Maritime Safety Agency and moved to the *kōdan*.

115

Table 8 (continued)

7. **Japan Railway Construction Corporation** (three-year term)
   President Shinohara Takeshi
   A doctor of engineering, Shinohara served as an official of the Ministry of Railways and the Ministry of Transportation from 1930 to 1961, retiring as head of the Railway Technology Research Institute. He served as an adviser to Yawata Steel before transferring to the *kōdan* in March 1970.

8. **New Tokyo International Airport Corporation** (four-year term)
   President Ōtsuka Shigeru
   An official of the former Ministry of Communications (Teishin-shō) and the Ministry of Posts and Telecommunications between 1935 and 1962, Ōtsuka retired as vice-minister of the Postal Ministry. He then served as a managing director of Japan Air Lines, vice-governor of Saitama Prefecture, and president of the airport *kōdan* as of July 1974.

9. **Keihin Port Development Authority** (four-year term)
   Chairman of the Board Minami Yoshio
   Minami was an official of the Ministry of Commerce and Industry between 1928 and 1949. Upon retirement he entered politics and was elected seven times to the House of Representatives. He was Minister of Transportation in the first Ikeda cabinet. After leaving politics he served as president of the Hokkaido Underground Resources Development Company, a special legal entity that existed from 1958 to 1968; and he headed the port *kōdan* from May 1969 to October 1975.

10. **Hanshin Port Development Authority** (four-year term)
    Chairman of the Board Hori Takeo
    The only *kōdan* president who was not a central government bureaucrat, Hori served as an official of the Osaka metropolitan government from 1923 to 1963.

11. **Japan Housing Corporation** (four-year term)
    President Nanbu Tetsuya
    Nanbu was an official of the Ministry of Welfare and the Ministry of Construction between 1940 and 1964. During his active duty, he worked for periods in the housing *kōko* and the housing *kōdan*. Upon retirement he was reemployed by the *kōdan*, and he became its president in April 1971.

12. **Japan Highway Public Corporation** (four-year term)
    President Maeda Mitsuyoshi
    An official of the Ministries of Home Affairs and Construction from 1940 to 1967, Maeda was vice-minister of Construction between January 7, 1965, and November 11, 1967. Upon retirement he served as vice-president of the highway corporation until June 1970, when he became president.

116

Table 8 (continued)

13. **Tokyo Expressway Public Corporation** (four-year term)
    Chairman of the Board Suzuki Shun'ichi
    A Home Ministry bureaucrat from 1934 to 1957, Suzuki retired as vice-minister of the Local Autonomy Agency. He served as vice-governor of Tokyo before taking up his *kōdan* position in June 1971.

14. **Hanshin Superhighway Corporation** (four-year term)
    Chairman of the Board Tenbō Hirohiko
    Tenbō served in the Railway Ministry from 1929 to 1951 and then became a vice-president of Japan National Railways. In 1956 he entered politics and was elected twice to the House of Councillors. In November 1971 he became head of the Hanshin highway *kōdan*.

15. **Honshu-Shikoku Bridge Authority** (four-year term)
    President Togashi Gaiichi
    A bureaucrat in the old Home Ministry and the Construction Ministry between 1929 and 1960, Togashi retired as chief engineer in the Ministry of Construction (June 1, 1958 to April 30, 1960). He then worked for Mitsubishi Realty Company, shifting in March 1962 to become vice-president of the Japan Highway Public Corporation. From 1966 to 1970 he was president of the highway *kōdan*. Upon completion of his term there he moved to the bridge *kōdan*, until he retired in July 1976.

Source: *Jinji kōshin roku* [Who's Who in Japan], 1975 and 1977 eds.

6
Government Corporations in the Energy Sector

Given Japan's unusual dearth of resources, the energy supply has been a subject of public policy since the Meiji Restoration of 1868; it has never been left entirely to the market or to private enterprise. Because of this, the events of 1973 and after—the OPEC oil embargo and price hikes, the growth of nationalism regarding resources around the world, and the threat of petroleum depletion—merely posed new problems for a government that has always been concerned with where the nation would get its energy. The key dates in Japanese energy history, prior to 1973, are 1886 for coal, when the Mining Bureau (Kōzan Kyoku) was set up within the Ministry of Agriculture and Commerce (the predecessor of the Ministry of Commerce and Industry and of MITI); 1911 for electricity, when the Electric Power Bureau within the Ministry of Communications (Teishin-shō Denki Kyoku) was given authority over the new Electrical Industry Law; and 1926 for petroleum, when the Mining Policy Section (Kōsei Ka) within the Mining Bureau was given responsibility for importing kerosene and for developing oil resources in North Sakhalin, as well as for expanding coal production.

The Japanese government took the lead in energy development, as in other areas of industrial policy, during the early Meiji period. It then withdrew somewhat for about the first three decades of the twentieth century in favor of private enterprise; in the 1930s it became directly involved in guiding and supervising a privately owned energy sector, and it has remained so to the present day. My concern in this chapter is with Japan's official energy policy from the late 1930s to the present. The problems of energy offer a good example of the government's approach to industrial guidance and of its use of numerous public corporations as instruments for executing official policies.

119

The basic story of Japanese energy is fairly easily told. Before the war, coal was the key to virtually every industrial activity in Japan, including the production of iron and steel and other metals, chemicals, cement, ceramics, glass, salt, paper, rayon pulp, processed foods, fertilizers, industrial gas, railway transportation, and thermally generated electricity. Most of this coal was mined domestically or in the colonies and the dependent areas of China. In 1930, Japan generated 14.6 percent of its electricity by burning coal (virtually all the rest was hydroelectric), a percentage which doubled to 29.8 percent by 1940. In the postwar period, thanks to Reconstruction Bank financing, coal production returned to the level of 1935 during 1949. By 1951, 21.5 percent of electricity was thermally generated, approaching prewar levels; by 1960 thermal power provided 49.4 percent, by 1965 60.4 percent, and by 1971 75.4 percent of all the country's electricity.[1]

By around 1960, however, it was no longer coal but oil that was firing the electric boilers. Coal had become a *shayō sangyō* (a "setting sun industry") during the late 1950s, even though the demand for electricity was rising prodigiously (between 1951 and 1970 the generation and use of electricity increased by some 758 percent). One authority calls the decline of coal "the greatest strategic retreat in the history of Japanese industry"; in light of the 1970s energy crisis, he also questions whether government pursued the proper policies toward coal.[2] The problem was that domestically mined coal cost so much more than imported petroleum. At first MITI fought to save the coal industry, and between 1955 and 1961 it had a measure of success. Inoue Makoto, in 1961 chief of the Coal Policy Section in MITI's Coal Bureau and later chief of the Public Utilities Bureau, believes that for a short period MITI managed to move coal's demise back about an hour, from 3:00 PM to 2:00 PM, on the industrial time clock.[3] But with the 280-day strike at the Miike shafts of Mitsui Mining in 1960, and the death of 458 miners in the Mikawa mine disaster of November 9, 1963, government's policy shifted to hastening coal's demise, even as it tried to prevent financial collapse for the coal industry.

Tables 9 and 10 record the results of government's changed coal policy. Between 1953 and 1973, the share of the nation's energy provided by domestic coal declined from 46.8 percent to 3.8 percent,

---

[1] Katō Takashi, *Shigen enerugī chō* [Natural Resources and Energy Agency] (Tokyo: Kyōiku Sha, 1974), p. 76.
[2] Maeda Yasuyuki, "Tsūshō sangyō seisaku no rekishi-teki tenkai" [The historical development of trade and industrial policy], *Tsūsan jyānaru*, May 25, 1975, p. 15.
[3] Sangyō Seisaku Kenkyū-jo [Industrial Policy Research Institute], ed., *Tsūsan-shō 20-nen gaishi* [An unofficial twenty-year history of MITI] (Tokyo: Sangyō Seisaku Kenkyū-jo, 1970), p. 76.

Table 9
JAPAN'S SOURCES OF ENERGY BETWEEN 1956 AND 1971
(percent)

Year	Petroleum	Hydroelectric	Coal	Other (including atomic)
1956	21.9	20.0	49.7	8.4
1965	58.4	11.3	27.3	3.0
1970	70.8	6.3	20.7	2.2
1971	73.5	6.7	17.5	2.3

Source: Katō Takashi, Shigen enerugī chō [Natural Resources and Energy Agency] (Tokyo: Kyōiku Sha, 1974), p. 15.

while petroleum's contribution jumped from 17.7 percent to 77.6 percent. At the same time, imports of coal for the steel industry and other industries that cannot use coal substitutes rose from slightly over 4 million tons in 1953 to 58 million tons in 1973. This meant that whereas the nation depended on imported fuels for 26.4 percent of its energy in 1961, that share climbed to 85.1 percent in 1974. 1961 was Japan's all-time peak year for coal production—almost 60 million tons were mined—but after that the government gradually reduced the number of active coal mines in Japan from about 800 to 36.[4]

Until what the Japanese call the "Fourth Middle Eastern War" of 1973, the petroleum industry was the reverse side of the coal coin. Between the cutthroat international oil competition following Suez and the Japanese liberalization of petroleum imports in 1962, oil undercut every effort to make the price of domestically produced coal competitive. In the decade between 1957 and 1967, the demand for refined petroleum products rose at a yearly rate of 19 percent. The effects on Japan were staggering—including unprecedented levels of air, land, and water pollution. The highest prewar yearly use of domestic and imported oil, primarily for the military, was 36 million kiloliters (approximately the same as the amount consumed in 1960).[5] The postwar low was 1 million kiloliters in 1947. After 1960, Japan's appetite for oil rose from 37 million kiloliters to over 318 million kiloliters in 1973, virtually all of it imported.

---

[4] Kojima Tsunehisa, "Sengo no sekitan seisaku to sekitan sangyō" [Postwar coal policy and the coal industry], Shosai no mado, no. 252 (April 1976), pp. 1-7.

[5] Katō, Shigen enerugī chō, p. 31.

Table 10
USE OF COAL VERSUS PETROLEUM, 1953–1973

Year	Coal National Production (thousands of tons)		Coal Imports (thousands of tons)		All Petroleum (Crude, Refined, LPG) (thousands of kl)	
1953	44,139	(46.8)	4,167	(6.0)	9,894	(17.7)
1954	43,223	(46.3)	3,167	(4.6)	10,497	(18.6)
1955	44,256	(44.8)	3,201	(4.4)	11,945	(20.2)
1956	50,821	(44.7)	4,195	(5.0)	14,903	(21.9)
1957	55,734	(42.7)	6,119	(6.5)	18,557	(24.1)
1958	51,273	(41.1)	4,447	(4.9)	18,948	(25.5)
1959	51,067	(36.5)	5,684	(5.5)	27,533	(32.7)
1960	57,459	(34.4)	8,704	(7.1)	37,422	(37.7)
1961	59,924	(31.3)	12,053	(8.6)	45,487	(39.9)
1962	57,549	(28.7)	10,826	(7.3)	55,347	(46.1)
1963	54,885	(24.0)	11,903	(7.0)	71,345	(51.8)
1964	56,174	(21.8)	13,982	(7.4)	85,728	(55.7)
1965	55,642	(19.1)	17,637	(8.2)	101,868	(58.4)
1966	56,032	(17.4)	20,796	(8.8)	117,352	(60.4)
1967	51,512	(14.4)	27,213	(10.2)	141,540	(64.6)
1968	50,460	(12.4)	34,185	(11.2)	166,633	(66.5)
1969	46,389	(10.5)	43,260	(12.3)	197,552	(68.3)
1970	40,851	(8.1)	50,941	(12.6)	235,027	(70.8)
1971	33,821	(6.3)	46,478	(11.2)	252,184	(73.5)
1972	28,083	(5.3)	50,506	(11.3)	276,547	(74.9)
1973	21,676	(3.8)	58,049	(11.7)	318,597	(77.6)

Note: Figures in parentheses are percentage of national energy requirements.
Source: MITI, *Tsūshō sangyō gyōsei shihan seiki no ayumi* [A quarter century of trade and industrial administration] (Tokyo: Tsūshō Sangyō Chōsa Kai, 1975), pp. 302–5.

Throughout this period of high-speed economic growth, MITI created policies and public corporations that not only subsidized the decline of coal but also controlled and kept as much as possible in national hands the ascent of petroleum. Electricity generation, yet a third responsibility of MITI's, mirrored and at the same time promoted the shift from coal to petroleum. As the demand for cheap electric power spiralled upward, MITI guided the companies producing it from hydrogeneration (SCAP's great enthusiasm) to thermal generation using coal, to thermal generation using oil, and finally toward nuclear power and the fast breeder reactor.

Lineage of the Public Corporations

The policies and politics, not to mention the lush growth of energy laws, that have accompanied these changes are extremely complex, but all of them involve government corporations. No assessment of Japan's energy policies in the 1970s can fail to take account of the activities of at least nine public corporations—including the Regional Promotion and Facilities Corporation (a *kōdan*), the Japan Petroleum Development Corporation (a *kōdan*), the Power Reactor and Nuclear Fuel Development Corporation (a *jigyōdan*), the Rationalization of Coal Industry Corporation (a *jigyōdan*), the Coal Mine Damage Corporation (a *jigyōdan*), the Electric Power Development Company (a special company), and the Coal for Electric Power Distribution Company (a special company). These corporations do not make policy. That is done within the ministries that create and control them: chiefly MITI's Natural Resources and Energy Agency, but also the Science and Technology Agency, the Economic Planning Agency, the Ministry of Finance, and the Ministry of Labor. However, once a policy has been hammered out, the chosen instrument of the government for administering it—that is, for investing some of the huge sums of the Fiscal Investment and Loan Plan—is normally an established or a newly created public corporation.

All of the major postwar public corporations in the energy sector have prewar precedents or ancestors. The lineage of the Japan Petroleum Development Corporation of 1967, for example, goes back to the Imperial Oil Company, a 50 percent government-owned special company created in 1941 and charged with the sole business of drilling for oil in areas the government designated. The Petroleum Resources Development Law of March 28, 1938 (law 31) empowered the Fuel Bureau of the Ministry of Commerce and Industry to promote active oil exploration by providing subsidies for test wells, and the Fuel Bureau set up the Imperial Oil Company to carry out this task. By the end of the war some eighteen stockholders held more than 80 percent of the stock available to the public (the Minister of Finance held 50 percent of the shares), and these stockholders received such benefits as guaranteed dividends and exemption from corporate taxes. Imperial Oil

123

expanded by absorbing the production departments of private oil companies until it controlled 90 percent of domestic oil production.[6]

SCAP continued the domestic search for oil, concentrating on the Yabase oil field in Akita prefecture, but it did not like the public-private arrangement the Imperial Oil Company represented. On February 8, 1949, the Holding Company Liquidation Commission designated Imperial Oil as an excessively concentrated concern; this designation was lifted on August 21, 1950, after the company had disposed of about 40 percent of the areas it held under prospecting leases. Finally, law 91 of April 1, 1950, eliminated all vestiges of government ownership, and Imperial became an independent oil company.

Meanwhile, however, the Japanese were working to convince SCAP that the functions of the old Imperial Oil Company needed to be continued. During 1951, the government and the occupation authorities collaborated to draft a law that would authorize the government to provide reimbursable subsidies for exploration, and aid for secondary recovery projects. The draft law also authorized a deliberation council (*shingikai*) to advise the MITI minister on oil policy. These proposals led to the setting up of the Petroleum and Natural Gas Development Council in 1952, after the occupation had ended, and the Petroleum Resources Development Company, a joint public-private special company, in 1955. The company's task was to explore for oil onshore and offshore in Japan, to see if any more oil were available than the 300,000 kiloliters per year being extracted during 1952 through 1955. The policies of both the deliberation council and the company were subject to the supervision and veto of the chief of MITI's Mining Bureau. Except for the existence of the deliberation council, which was a long-term planning body, the Petroleum Resources Development Company was the equivalent of the old Imperial Oil Company, including its use of private as well as government capital—a point Japanese analysts readily concede.[7]

After Suez, as the country's demand for oil swelled, the Petroleum Resources Development Company gave up on domestic exploration and began investing in Japanese overseas enterprises such as the Arabian Oil Company and the North Sumatra Petroleum Development Company. However, with demand burgeoning for all kinds of new petroleum products, including those used by the petrochemical industry, the need

[6] Supreme Commander for the Allied Powers, Monograph 41, "The Petroleum Industry," *Historical Monographs* (Washington, D.C.: National Archives, 1951), pp. 34-37.

[7] Nihon Chōki Shin'yō Ginkō [Japan Long-term Credit Bank], *Jūyō sangyō sengo nijūgo nenshi* [The history of important industries during the twenty-five postwar years] (Tokyo: Sangyō to Keizai, 1972), pp. 82-83.

for much larger overseas investments became apparent. MITI therefore set up an internal Oil Kōdan Establishment Preparation Office, and the officials of this office drafted the law that created the Japan Petroleum Development Corporation (law 99 of July 29, 1967).

The Japan Petroleum Development Corporation, a *kōdan*, replaced the Petroleum Resources Development Company, a joint public-private special company, and it began investing funds from the Fiscal Investment and Loan Plan in overseas oil projects (some ¥50.2 billion in 1973). With offices in Beirut, Washington, London, and Houston, as well as Tokyo, the JPDC is both a government finance corporation for making loans to oil developers, and the government's leading technological and geological research institute in the petroleum field. It is controlled by the Development Section, Petroleum Department, of MITI's Natural Resources and Energy Agency; and its chief executive officer, Shimada Yoshito, is a former chief of MITI's Enterprises Bureau, the number-two man after the vice-minister in the ministry's pecking order.[8]

Oil Refining and Distribution Companies

Continuity between prewar and postwar practices is not quite so clear-cut in the area of petroleum refining and distribution as it is in crude oil exploration. Before the war, there were three types of refineries in Japan. First were the military refineries at Yokkaichi and Iwakuni (run by the army) and at Tokuyama (run by the navy). These refineries imported their own crude oil from army-controlled areas in the south seas and from navy-controlled fields in North Sakhalin. In principle, the military was subject to the allocation authority of the General Mobilization Bureau and the Fuel Bureau of the Ministry of Munitions, but in practice it ignored the civilian government. Second were the civilian refineries on the Japan Sea coast that processed domestic crude; third were the civilian refineries on the Pacific Ocean coast that processed imported crude for the civilian market. The last were organized into control associations under the Fuel Bureau; this structure was perpetuated under the occupation, except that the control associations were replaced by a single government corporation, the Petroleum Distribution Kōdan, on April 14, 1947. Until July 1949, SCAP banned the import of crude oil, and the Pacific coast refineries were idle. After that Japan began to import Middle Eastern oil in joint ventures with the international oil companies.

---

[8] For the views of former MITI vice-minister Ōjimi Yoshihisa on the JPDC, see Organization for Economic Cooperation and Development, *The Industrial Policy of Japan* (Paris: OECD, 1972), p. 59.

Oil did not flow freely into Japan, however. On December 1, 1949, the Foreign Exchange and Foreign Trade Control Law (law 228) came into effect, giving MITI absolute control over the use of all "foreign means of payment." Until the liberalization of Japan's oil policy in 1962, the International Trade Bureau of MITI concentrated all foreign exchange into a single account, which it then allocated to private traders in accordance with the ministry's overall schemes for rapid industrial development.[9] Domestic oil refiners and distributors were not necessarily favored under this system, since most of them were closely connected with the international (usually American) oil giants. Only in the late 1950s, with the decline of coal and the substitution of oil for industrial use, did MITI begin to allow large amounts of Japan's foreign currency budget to be used for oil.[10] But, of course, as the demand for oil in Japan rose, so did the pressure from the international oil companies for an end to currency controls.

In 1962 Japan "liberalized" oil imports, but it simultaneously enacted the Petroleum Industry Law, which requires the permission of the MITI minister for virtually every decision a private oil company makes. Nakagawa Riichirō, chief of the Mining Bureau from June 15, 1968 to November 7, 1969, maintains that there is no real difference between the old foreign currency allocation system and the present industry law system.[11] Under both, MITI makes estimates of the annual demand for various petroleum products and allocates either foreign exchange (before 1962) or approvals of investment and business plans (after 1962) in order to meet its targets. There is one difference, however. Under the old system MITI had a clear legal authority to guide the industry, whereas under the new system it must rely on "administrative guidance." During 1962 and 1963, Idemitsu Petroleum defied MITI's advice that the whole industry should curtail production, a move that led to a price war and ultimately worsened all the refiners' financial

---

[9] On the International Trade Bureau, see Chalmers Johnson, "MITI and Japanese International Economic Policy," in Robert A. Scalapino, ed., *The Foreign Policy of Modern Japan* (Berkeley and Los Angeles: University of California Press, 1977), pp. 227-79.

[10] Allocations of oil during the 1950s were intensely political, and old MITI petroleum officials often tell stories of the pressures they were under to respond favorably to some powerful pressure group. The most prominent instance was the pressure brought by the National Federation of Fishing Cooperatives (Zengyoren) to ensure that fishermen in the Northeast got their allocation of motor fuel. The Diet leaders of the fishing lobby—Suzuki Zenkō of Iwate prefecture, Shirahama Nikichi of Nagasaki, and Chida Tadashi of Iwate—loved to call the MITI minister and lesser officials before their committee to complain to them about the shortages and prices of oil. The fishermen's lobby won this struggle. See *Tsūsan-shō 20-nen gaishi*, p. 129.

[11] Ibid., pp. 131-32.

positions. After about 1965 the companies and MITI developed a harmonious working relationship (some Japanese critics believe too harmonious) which lasted until the oil crisis of 1973, when the system was reformed again in favor of a much more active MITI role.[12]

Another feature of the liberalized era was MITI's creation of the Kyōdō Oil Company as a counterfoil to the international majors (discussed in chapter 2). The ministry also placed *amakudari* officials on the boards of directors of all but a few oil firms doing business in Japan, to ensure the companies' responsiveness to administrative guidance.[13] In general, the system of controls over refining and distribution has a family resemblance to the control cartels of the prewar and wartime periods, except that the government's voice is if anything more prominent today than it was then.

The Coal Companies

Government's policy toward the coal companies has varied in several respects from the general pattern we have seen in petroleum. The prewar, wartime, and occupation policies were similar: the wartime coal control companies became the coal distribution *kōdan* during the occupation, and coal production was subsidized and given top priority under the Economic Stabilization Board–Reconstruction Finance Bank structure. The greatest change in the coal business since the war was its loss of about one third of its labor force when SCAP repatriated some 130,000 forcibly employed Korean and Chinese miners. The government and the zaibatsu owners of the coal mines did not begin effectively to recruit Japanese replacements until SCAP ordered that food and other supplemental rations be supplied to coal miners. In June 1948, occupation officials concluded that the mines had been rehabilitated mechanically to their prewar condition.[14] However, the price of coal and the wages of the workers still were subsidized by the government until late in 1949, when SCAP ordered the Coal Distribution Kōdan abolished. Then the real problems started.

---

[12] See Nihon Keizai Seisaku Gakkai [Japan Economic Policy Association], ed., *Shigen mondai to keizai seisaku* [Resources problems and economic policy] (Tokyo: Keisō Shobō, 1976), pp. 7-39; and Okamoto Ryūzō, *Sekiyu gyōkai* [The petroleum industry] (Tokyo: Kyōiku Sha, 1975).

[13] See list of almost fifty ex-MITI oil company executives, in *Asahi shimbun*, morning ed., April 16, 1974, p. 3; reprinted in Watanabe Yōzō, "Sekiyu sangyō to sengo keizaihō taisei" [The petroleum industry and the postwar structure of economic law], in Tokyo University Social Science Research Institute, *Sengo kaikaku* [Postwar reform] (Tokyo: Tokyo Daigaku Shakai Kagaku Kenkyū-jo, 1975), vol. 8, p. 275.

[14] SCAP, Monograph 45, "Coal," *Historical Monographs*, pp. 6-23.

Most authorities date the onset of the post-independence coal crisis from the long Tanrō (Japan Coal Miners' Union) strike that began in October 1952. Under free market conditions the supply of coal had become unreliable, and strikes were causing prices to shoot up. During 1953, the consumption of heavy fuel oil rose proportionately. Also, the mine owners seemed unable to wean themselves from the subsidies and government investments of the wartime and occupation eras.

Immediately following the end of the occupation, the government enacted the Temporary Coal Mine Damage Rehabilitation Law (law 295 of August 1, 1952), which established local and regional public corporations (*jigyōdan*) for making official capital available to repair mines and to prevent environmental damage. In 1963, these local bodies were united into a single governmental special legal entity, a "fund" or *kikin*, and in 1968 MITI converted the fund into a corporation, the Coal Mine Damage Corporation (Sekitan Kōgai Jigyōdan).[15] In 1975, this government corporation was still in existence, and it controlled a budget of about ¥11 billion. The chairman of its board in 1975 was Sanuki Kihachi, a MITI official between 1935 and 1958 and a former chief of the Coal Bureau. From 1952 to the 1970s all the leading coal companies—Mitsui, Hokkaido, Meiji, Taiheiyō, Matsushima, and Nittetsu—were recipients of its aid.

Still, by 1955 none of the coal companies was able to show a profit, and MITI decided that something drastic had to be done about what the whole country was calling "the coal mess."[16] The ministry chose to implement a policy of "rationalization" of the coal industry: in practice this meant forcing inefficient medium and small operators to close or to merge with larger firms in order to increase production, achieve economies of scale, and reduce labor costs. The government offered to bear the costs of closing low-productivity mines, and to subsidize the price of coal to make it competitive with oil.

The primary author of these measures was Kojima Keizō, in 1955 head of the Coal Policy Section (Tansei Ka) in MITI's Coal Bureau. His section's efforts resulted in the enactment of the Coal Mining Rationalization Special Measures Law (law 156 of August 10, 1955), which in turn authorized creation of the Coal Mining Facilities Cor-

---

15 The Mine Damage Compensation Fund (Kōgai Baishō Kikin) was established on July 1, 1963. On May 1, 1965, its name was changed to Mine Damage Fund (Kōgai Kikin); and on July 1, 1968 it was upgraded into the *jigyōdan*. For the text of the original 1952 law and of related coal statutes, see MITI, *Tsūshō sangyō roppō* [Compendium of trade and industry laws] (Tokyo: Tsūshō Sangyō Chōsakai, 1974 ed.), pp. 1167-83. Another useful source for some of the laws related to the corporations discussed in this chapter is Kokudo-chō [National Land Agency], *Kokudo roppō* (Tokyo: Shin Nihon Hōki Shuppan K.K., 1975).
16 *Tsūsan-shō 20-nen gaishi*, p. 71.

poration (Sekitan Kōgyō Seibi Jigyōdan), which actually supplied the funds for liquidating mines and paying off miners who were let go. Kojima described his plan for the rationalization of coal as one of "scrap and build," although later critics have charged that "scrap" actually meant destroying Japan's indigenous coal industry, and "build" meant building up the profits of the ex-zaibatsu firms such as Mitsui.[17] Regardless of how it turned out, however, the intent of the policy in 1955 was to save the coal industry and restrict the petroleum industry.

During that same year the Diet passed the intensely controversial Heavy Oil Boiler Control Law, which put a duty on imported fuel oil. It is said that Tanaka Kakuei, then chairman of the lower house's Commerce Committee and later both MITI minister and prime minister, cleared the bill through his committee while its opponents were in the rest room.[18] Along with Kojima's measures, this law revived the coal industry and restrained the move to oil for about three years.

During 1957 a short but sharp recession increased the industrial demand for a cheap source of energy, and the worldwide overproduction of oil following Suez provided the supply. The full effects of what the Japanese call the "energy revolution" began to be felt during 1958 and 1959. To meet the oil challenge, MITI's Coal Bureau lowered the price of coal and intensified its "scrap and build" policy. On September 1, 1960, the Coal Mining Facilities Corporation was reorganized and renamed the Rationalization of the Coal Industry Corporation (Sekitan Kōgyō Gōrika Jigyōdan), with augmented price subsidies and government funds for reemploying dismissed miners, buying up mining rights, and so forth. In 1961, the corporation began to subsidize the Ministry of Labor's Employment Promotion Projects Corporation (Koyō Sokushin Jigyōdan), set up that year to find new jobs for coal miners and other workers who had been laid off because of technical or rationalization developments.

The early 1960s saw the crisis of coal emerge in full force. The trade unions fought back against the rationalization measures, which resulted in long strikes and lock-outs throughout the coal fields and bitter disputes in the Diet. Some political leaders, Kōno Ichirō for example, called for the nationalization of coal; and MITI, in response, gradually shifted away from trying to save the coal industry. Instead, MITI worked to alleviate the social dislocations caused by mine closings, miners' leaving even the productive mines in the wake of a series of lethal mine disasters, and the depression that was spreading through-

---

17 For Kojima's role, see ibid. For an informed criticism of the policy, see Kojima Tsunehisa, *Shosai no mado*, April 1976, pp. 5-6.
18 *Tsūsan-shō 20-nen gaishi*, p. 130.

out the coal fields of Kyushu. The ministry's most important new venture was the Coal Mine Area Rehabilitation Corporation (Santan Chiiki Shinkō Jigyōdan), set up on July 20, 1962. Its mission was to build industrial parks in old coal-producing areas and to provide incentives to nonmining industries to move there.

Even with these measures, the government did not give up completely on trying to shore up the domestic coal industry until about 1966. A series of blue-ribbon committees headed by the venerable professor and MITI adviser Arisawa Hiromi (creator of the priority production policy for coal during the occupation) called for production levels of 55 million tons annually as a matter of national security. However, in 1966 the government decided it could no longer afford the subsidies at this level of production. In that year it lowered the coal production target to 50 million tons (cut in January 1968 to 36 million tons), assumed the debts of the coal companies up to a total of ¥100 billion, and raised the price stabilization subsidies. To pay for all of this it put a 12 percent tariff on imported petroleum, of which 10 percent was to be deposited in a new Coal Special Account for the use of the coal policy corporations. The duty and the account persist to the present day; but the biggest recipients from the account are not only the Coal Mine Area Rehabilitation Corporation but the Japan Petroleum Development Corporation as well. During fiscal year 1973, the Coal Special Account netted about ¥135 billion, of which MITI's Natural Resources and Energy Agency spent ¥108 billion for coal-related policies and ¥26 billion for petroleum development.[19]

As it turned out, the policy of extensively subsidizing the coal industry in lieu of nationalizing it was so inefficient that by 1973 the government was doing everything it could to close down the coal industry altogether and use the oil tariff receipts for more productive purposes. By the time of the "oil shock" of late 1973, domestic coal had become negligible in Japan's energy supply. Even after the shock, government emphasized diversification abroad rather than a revival of the Kyushu mines. Most of the miners had long since gone into other lines of work, and many of them had moved to the cities.

The policies government designed in response to "the coal mess" have been adapted since then to deal with the 1970s problems of environmental pollution, the need for rational land use, overcrowding in the Tokyo-Osaka industrial zone, and the virtual depopulation of some rural areas as residents move to the cities (what the Japanese call the

---

[19] Katō, *Shigen enerugī chō*, p. 42; MITI, *Tsūshō sangyō gyōsei shihan seiki no ayumi* [A quarter century of trade and industrial administration] (Tokyo: Tsūshō Sangyō Chōsa Kai, 1975), p. 55.

kaso-kamitsu problem). In October 1969, Konaga Keiichi, one of MITI's more able officials, became chief of the Industrial Location Guidance Section in the ministry's Enterprises Bureau (Kigyō Kyoku Ritchi Shidō Ka). He organized a team of three or four people and wrote a grand design for the dispersal of factories throughout Japan, a policy that was also intended to ease urban pollution, soaring land prices, and the housing shortage. Konaga's ideas came to the attention of Tanaka Kakuei, when he became MITI minister on July 5, 1971; and Tanaka incorporated them into his own highly publicized "Plan for the Reform of the Japanese Archipelago" (*Nihon rettō kaizō an*), which he popularized during his prime ministership, July 7, 1972 to December 9, 1974. While Tanaka was prime minister he had Konaga transferred from MITI to be his private secretary.[20]

The concrete results of the Konaga-Tanaka scheme were the Industrial Relocation Promotion Law of June 16, 1972 (law 73) and the upgrading of the Coal Mine Area Rehabilitation Corporation of 1962, a *jigyōdan*, into the Industrial Relocation and Coal Production Areas Promotion Corporation (Kōgyō Saihaichi Santan Chiiki Shinkō Kōdan), a *kōdan*, on November 2, 1972. On August 1, 1974, the new *kōdan* was renamed again, to emphasize its new functions rather than its origins as a welfare agency for coal-mining regions: it is now called the Regional Promotion and Facilities Corporation (Chiiki Shinkō Setsubi Kōdan). It still has major offices in the Kyushu and Hokkaido coal fields and spends funds from the Coal Special Account, but its more important duties are land-use planning, new town development, building parks and roads, and lending funds to firms that want to relocate out of the Tokyo-Osaka area. The corporation is now controlled jointly by MITI, the National Land Agency (also a Tanaka creation), and the Ministry of Construction, and it is one of Japan's most important institutions for social engineering. Thus, even though the coal industry is now dead, the public corporations created to deal with its problems are alive and thriving.

The Battle of Electric Power

The electric power industry has followed a very different pattern of public policies and public corporations from the petroleum and coal industries. Three factors make electricity different. First, the industry itself originated in the Meiji era as a private enterprise, and electrical

---

[20] Kusayanagi Daizō, "Tsūsan-shō: tamesareru sutā kanchō" [MITI: a star bureaucracy under fire], *Bungei shunjū*, August 1974, pp. 118-19; and Seisaku Jihō Sha, ed., *Nihon no kanchō* [Japanese government agencies] (Tokyo: Seisaku Jihō Sha, 1974), under "MITI," p. 277.

131

entrepreneurs have always been among the strongest and most outspoken opponents of governmental controls. Second, the demand for more electrical power in the postwar world has been close to insatiable, meaning that the need for investment funds—as well as for low rates for consumers—has exceeded even the resources of the Fiscal Investment and Loan Plan. And third, despite the near nationalization of the electric power industry in the 1930s, the government remains only one participant in this industry, facing equally strong industrial and political interests. None of this means that the industry is unregulated or that public corporations play no part in it, only that the electrical industry has developed differently from industries that have been directly fostered by the government or in which the *zaikai* is less talented or less well organized.

Between 1937 and 1941, there occurred in Japan one of the great battles of modern times over the control of a key industry. Militarists and reform bureaucrats, wanting to increase rapidly the power-generating capacity of the nation and being ideologically opposed to the idea of privately owned public utilities, fought against five major zaibatsu-dominated electric power companies that were adamantly opposed to turning over their businesses to bureaucrats. Private electric power had been under government regulation since 1911 (and earlier in terms of safety codes), and the industry had been self-controlled and cartelized since the Electric Enterprise Law of April 2, 1931 (law 61). But the industry also had long been known for its vigorous competition, fragmentation, and devotion to profit. The numerous private and municipal electric companies cooperated only with difficulty on large-scale generation and transmission projects. The rural areas—where the depression hit the hardest, and whose misery was of great concern to the militarists—remained unelectrified. Small businesses too seemed to be at the mercy of the power companies, for they were almost totally dependent on the supply of cheap electricity. Thus, with the rise of militarism and totalitarian ideologies during the late 1930s, many generals and bureaucrats were predisposed to take over electric power and make it part of a "national defense state."

In January 1937, the so-called Tanomogi draft law for the control of electricity (named after the minister of communications in the Hirota cabinet) was introduced in the Diet. It called for private ownership but state management of the electrical industry, and for government-directed investments in electric power projects to increase the overall supply and lower the price of power to military industries. Amid contending charges of zaibatsu selfishness on the one hand and Bolshevik tendencies on the other, civilian politicians beat back this proposal.

However, the first Konoe cabinet took up the same problem six months later, with greater care and with a new urgency supplied by the outbreak of war with China in July. Communications Minister Nagai Ryūtarō involved electrical industry leaders themselves in a "Temporary Electric Power Investigation Association" and forced them to draft their own state control bill. This so-called Nagai draft passed the Diet in March 1938.

The new law differed from the Tanomogi draft in that it left management and ownership in private hands, but it called for a joint public-private special company which would construct new thermal and hydro generating plants and transmission lines, and which would sell power to the private companies. Called the Japan Electric Power Generation and Transmission Company (Nippon Hassōden K.K.), the new company was an excellent example of the compromises the military and private interests made in this period through the device of the national policy company. Together with Japan Steel, Hassōden became a key prewar domestic national policy company. The Electric Power Control Law (number 76 of 1938) also created an Electric Power Agency (Denki-chō) as an external agency of the Ministry of Communications to mediate between Hassōden and the private companies. By the time of the Pacific War, however, the Electric Power Agency and Hassōden had so expanded their activities that the electric power industry was, in effect, nationalized.[21]

Hassōden absorbed some thirty-three private companies and commenced operations on April 1, 1939. The director general of the Electric Power Agency named the president and vice-president of Hassōden and had the power to approve all members of the board of directors nominated by the participating companies. Through what was essentially a state-supervised merger rather than an outright nationalization, the government brought under its control capital assets worth some ¥5 billion (at the prewar value of the yen), or exactly 25 percent of the total corporate capital in Japan.[22] The importance of this action for the long-range rationalization of the Japanese industrial structure cannot be overstated. Although private industry was cool to Hassōden for obvious reasons and the militarists were only interested in increasing war-making potential, postwar Japan benefited from the large-scale operations and nationwide investments that the reduction of thirty-three companies to one made possible.

21 For the history of electric power administration in Japan, see Ōsawa Etsuji, *Denryoku jigyōkai* [The electric power industry] (Tokyo: Kyōiku Sha, 1975), pp. 197-216.
22 Itō Mitsuharu, "Munitions Unlimited—The Controlled Economy," *The Japan Interpreter*, vol. 7, nos. 3-4 (Summer-Autumn 1972), p. 355.

Hassōden and the Haiden

During the summer of 1941 and into early 1942, as part of the movement to create control associations, the government took over some seventy electricity marketing companies and reorganized them into nine regional electricity distributing public policy companies called Haiden. Hassōden and the nine Haiden companies controlled over 83 percent of the nation's power facilities by the end of World War II. However, during and immediately after the war, the government considered electric power to be a "basic industry," not a "public utility." No more than 10 percent of the total electricity generated during 1943 (the year of peak production) went to household customers. In the immediate postwar years, electricity continued to be rationed not only for households but also for use in electric boilers, salt production processes, and electrical advertising. Just as Japan uses more of its petroleum for industry than for transportation, it also uses more of its electricity for industry than for household consumption, today as in the past.

Another wartime development of postwar importance was the transfer of ministerial authority over electric power to the MITI line of succession. When the Ministry of Munitions was set up in November 1943, it took over the Communications Ministry's Electric Power Agency. After the war, the Munitions Ministry's successors, the Ministry of Commerce and Industry (1945–1949) and MITI (1949 to the present), retained electric power within their jurisdiction. The postwar equivalent of the old Electric Power Agency, including most of its traditions and many of its personnel, is the Public Utilities Bureau of MITI.

On February 22, 1948, the occupation-created Holding Company Liquidation Commission declared that the Hassōden company and the nine regional electricity distribution companies constituted an excessive concentration of economic power. "An undesirable bureaucratic relationship existed, in the opinion of SCAP, between the Government and the privately owned companies as represented in the top ranks of the officials of the electric power industry, requiring many of them to 'serve two masters.' "[23] The commission's findings set off a battle within Japanese industrial, political, and bureaucratic circles that lasted until 1952, one that rivaled the fights in the Diet back when the Electric Power Control Law was first passed in 1938.

In May 1948, as part of its new policy to get the Japanese economy back on its feet, SCAP appointed a wholly American "Deconcentration

---

[23] SCAP, Monograph 25, "Deconcentration of Economic Power," *Historical Monographs*, p. 79.

134

Review Board" (DRB) to go over the actions of the Japanese Holding Company Liquidation Commission and make sure its decisions were not hampering economic recovery. The DRB lifted the orders to deconcentrate many major enterprises, but it had trouble with the order to break up electric power. Basically, the DRB agreed with SCAP and the commission that the Hassōden-Haiden complex was an undemocratic, government-dominated cartel, but it did not know what to do about it. Therefore, on July 11, 1949, after meeting with the minister of international trade and industry, the DRB ordered Japan to create an American-style "Public Utilities Commission," which was to break up the old system and replace it with a civilian power industry. On August 3, 1949, the DRB went out of existence, and the Supreme Commander asserted that the board's orders marked the end of the occupation's efforts to "democratize the Japanese economy on a peacetime basis."[24] From then on it was up to the Japanese.

Throughout the rest of 1949 and all of 1950, the Diet debated interminably what the proposed Public Utilities Commission was supposed to do and who was to be a member of it. Industry wanted cheap power; company owners wanted to make a return on their capital; the bureaucracy was interested in keeping its sphere of influence intact— and all had political representatives in the Diet. SCAP followed this debate closely, for the health of the electric power industry was vital to Japanese progress toward economic independence, and the Americans were supplying large amounts of counterpart funds to Japan for investment in new hydroelectric projects. By the autumn of 1950, after the outbreak of the Korean War had made Japan's recovery even more important, the Diet had still failed even to set up the Public Utilities Commission. SCAP wrote that, "Current (October 1950) news reports reveal that undercover political maneuvering of an unsavory nature has surrounded the Japanese action."[25]

As a result, on December 15, 1950, SCAP intervened directly and had the Yoshida government issue two so-called Potsdam Ordinances— that is, cabinet orders that carried the force of law because they were based on Japan's acceptance of SCAP's absolute authority following the surrender of 1945. These cabinet orders (numbers 342 and 343 of 1950) dissolved Hassōden and the nine Haiden companies and created the Public Utilities Commission as their receivers. The use of the Potsdam device so late in the occupation and over a matter of such major financial importance created a furor in Japan. Sometime later,

24 Ibid., p. 83.
25 SCAP, Monograph 46, "Expansion and Reorganization of the Electric Power and Gas Industries," *Historical Monographs*, p. 44.

Yokoo Shigemi, who had been the MITI minister in late 1950, commented about the electric power ordinances that General MacArthur had not only ordered their issuance but also drafted their contents.[26]

The key figure on the new Public Utilities Commission was Matsunaga Yasuzaemon, president since 1928 of the Tōhō Electric Company and universally regarded as both the father and the brains (*shunō*) of Japan's modern electrical industry. Matsunaga was a veteran of the wars against the bureaucrats in the late 1930s, and he was a champion of the private utility business. But he also recognized that Japan's industry was going to need a lot of electricity, and that the funds to produce it would have to come from official as well as private sources. Therefore, he produced a structure that was something of a compromise. He abolished Hassōden (temporarily, as we shall see) and created nine independent electric power companies that differed from the Haiden in that they were fully integrated generating, transmitting, and distributing enterprises. All of them—Tokyo, Chūbu (Nagoya), Kansai (Osaka), Chūgoku (Hiroshima), Hokuriku (Toyama), Tōhoku (Sendai), Shikoku (Takamatsu), Kyushu (Fukuoka), and Hokkaido (Sapporo)—came into existence on May 1, 1951. SCAP had wanted only seven companies, and in 1957 Matsunaga himself declared that some of the companies were too weak financially to stand on their own (he wanted to merge Tokyo with Tōhoku, and Kansai with Chūbu). However, the political interests of various regions and the power of the Haiden precedent prevailed, and Japan got nine regional electric companies, all of which exist today.

The EPDC

Immediately after the occupation ended, the Japanese government abolished the Public Utilities Commission and transferred its duties to the Public Utilities Bureau of MITI. It also created, on September 16, 1952, the Electric Power Development Company (EPDC) (Dengen Kaihatsu K.K.), a special company jointly owned by the government (which held 74 percent of the fixed capital as of 1975) and the nine companies (which held 26 percent). The EPDC builds power-generating and transmission facilities, and it supplies electricity to the electric companies. Without exactly admitting that it is a postwar re-creation of Hassōden, old MITI electric power bureaucrats say they prefer its world to that of the nine companies, where their influence and regulatory power are weaker. Iwatake Teruhiko, chief of the Public Utilities

---

[26] Harry Emerson Wildes, *Typhoon in Tokyo: The Occupation and Its Aftermath* (New York: Macmillan Co., 1954), p. 121.

Bureau from June 8, 1956 to June 15, 1957, calls the EPDC a "legitimate child" but characterizes the nine companies as children by a "forced adoption," referring of course to SCAP's role in their birth.[27] Whatever its parentage, the EPDC is one of the most important of all the *tokushu hōjin* in postwar Japan.

In 1952, the EPDC began its operations by making major investments in hydroelectric projects. The development of hydroelectric power had been SCAP's preferred strategy for enlarging Japan's generating capacity, despite the lack of large rivers in Japan, and EPDC merely carried on that work. Only two years after its creation, however, EPDC gave up on any new hydroelectric dams and turned instead to building modern thermal electric generating plants. To do this it had to import foreign technology: the Long Term Credit Bank notes that the heat efficiency of the best Japanese plant built in 1952 was 5.1 percent, whereas American firms were then manufacturing plants with very large capacities and with efficiencies of 33 percent.[28] During 1952 and 1953, the Kyushu, Kansai, and Chūbu companies, plus the EPDC, imported such modern plants, using World Bank loans to supplement their inadequate government funds. The proceeds of the surplus agricultural products deals (mentioned in chapter 4) also went in part for this purpose. By 1973, the thermal revolution was complete; the Tokyo Electric Power Company, for example, which is the world's largest private power company, produced 16.8 percent of its 19,071,000 kilowatts during that year by hydroelectric generation, 80.8 percent by thermal generation, and 2.4 percent by atomic reactor generation.[29]

The EPDC is more a public corporation and less an extension of the bureaucracy than most of the special legal entities. Its first president was Takasaki Tatsunosuke, a prominent politician, successor during the war to Aiyukawa Gisuke as head of Manchurian Heavy Industries, and the father of the ad hoc Sino-Japanese trade agreements during the early 1960s. Often the EPDC has been caught up in political turmoil, and it occasionally has been accused of corruption. For example, a group of journalists who cover MITI charge that Utsumi Kiyoharu was named president of the EPDC in 1956 primarily because he was trusted by the leaders of the Liberal Democratic Party. They knew he would not reveal the Hazama Construction Company's

---

27 Iwatake Teruhiko, *Zuihitsu toranomon* [Jottings at Toranomon] (Tokyo: Tsūshō Sangyō Chōsakai, 1960), p. 87. (Toranomon is the place in Tokyo where MITI's headquarters is located.)
28 Nihon Chōki Shin'yō Ginkō, *Jūyō sangyō*, p. 6.
29 "Corporate Analysis: The Tokyo Electric Power Co., Inc.," *Japan Times*, December 18, 1973, p. 10.

overcharges to EPDC for building the Sakuma Dam in the early 1950s, nor the fact that Hazama had made major campaign contributions to such Liberal Democratic leaders as Ōno Bamboku and Kōno Ichirō.[30]

MITI has always fought to protect and preserve the EPDC as part of its jurisdiction against the encroachments of other ministries. The issue of jurisdiction arose most critically when the question of developing atomic power came up in Japan. Since the original law creating the EPDC gave the company duties primarily in the hydroelectric area, it has always been in danger of losing its raison d'être; the Administrative Management Agency once proposed the EPDC's abolition since there were no more hydroelectric sites to develop. In 1956 and 1957, the Japanese government entered the nuclear generation field and set up the Atomic Energy Bureau within the Science and Technology Agency (STA) to promote nuclear reactors. MITI responded by sending its own officers to the STA to head the Atomic Energy Bureau and to ensure that the EPDC had a role to play in reactor investments. Today, the EPDC is a major investor in the Japan Atomic Power Company, a private (type V) company jointly owned by the EPDC and the nine electric companies, and in the Power Reactor and Nuclear Fuel Development Corporation, a special legal entity controlled by the Atomic Energy Bureau of the Science and Technology Agency. The EPDC has successfully negotiated the transitions from water-generated electricity to steam generation using coal, to steam generation using oil, and to conventional and fast breeder reactors. Today it is the major coordinating and development arm for the whole electric power industry.

The institutions for administering electric power in Japan, like all institutions everywhere, mirror their complex histories. The electric companies themselves, despite their independence and wealth, show many traces of both Hassōden and the Matsunaga era. For example, the wife of Yokoyama Michio, chairman of the board in 1973 of Chūbu Electric, is the niece of Matsunaga Yasuzaemon himself. Chairman Ashihara Yoshishige and President Yoshimura Seizō of Kansai Electric both began their careers in the Kansai Haiden, and chairman Hirai Kan'ichirō of Tōhoku Electric was a former director of Hassōden (he was also a vice-president of the EPDC in the early 1960s). In 1951, Hirai served as the chief technical officer of the Public Utilities Commission under Matsunaga. Both the Tokyo and Kansai companies have former MITI vice-ministers on their boards of directors; and the chairman of Hokkaido Electric in 1973 was the vice-minister of commerce

---

[30] Tsūsan-shō Kisha Kurabu [MITI Journalists' Club], *Tsūsan-shō* [MITI] (Tokyo: Hōbunsha, 1958), pp. 222-31.

138

and industry in 1947 and 1948. At the EPDC itself, the president from 1970 to 1975 was Ōbori Hiromu, an old MITI career official and a former director of the Public Utilities Bureau. Ōbori is credited with being the successor to Matsunaga as the "brains" of the electric power industry. His replacement as president after April 30, 1975, was Morozumi Yoshihiko, one of MITI's most illustrious vice-ministers.[31] Thus, the ties among all nine companies, the EPDC, MITI, and the political world, as well as back in time to Hassōden and the occupation, bind the whole industry together and make it impossible to say whether it belongs to the public, the private, or the public corporate sector.

Conclusions

In this chapter I have tried to illustrate some of the important functions that public corporations perform in one segment of Japanese life. Further examples could be found in almost any other area of the economy or society. One reason for dwelling on the histories and manifold activities of public energy corporations is to try to dispel any impression that may have been left by the previous chapter that public corporations are merely retirement havens, or that they are created only to expand the jurisdictions of the central government ministries. *Amakudari,* bureaucratic competition, political influence, and so forth are all problems of Japanese governmental administration, but they are problems that are fully acknowledged by Japanese leaders and citizens and that are the subject of continual reform movements. In discussing them in this study, my intent is to present accurately the state of public corporate activity, not merely to criticize or expose. Practices such as "descent from heaven" are probably just as common, but less systematic and acknowledged, in countries such as the United States—though in the United States the process probably should be called "ascent to heaven." [32] The energy sector illustrates that whatever problems there may be with public corporations in Japan, they are entrusted with the most vital activities for the continued functioning of the Japanese system, and their corruption or failure is rare.

---

31 Shigen Kaihatsu Un'ei Chōsakai [Resources Development Management Investigation Council], ed., *Zaikaijin jiten* [Dictionary of business leaders] (Tokyo: Shigen Kaihatsu Un'ei Chōsakai, 1973), pp. 7-25.
32 On the United States, see *Serving Two Masters: A Common Cause Study of Conflicts of Interest in the Executive Branch* (Washington, D.C.: Common Cause, 1976), 74 pp.

7

The Public Corporations and
Bureaucratism

An editorial entitled "Streamlining the Bureaucracy" in the *Japan Times Weekly* of March 5, 1977, contained these observations:

> As for public corporations, a more stringent review system should be established to evaluate the performance of each corporation on a periodic basis. Is there any valid reason why a corporation not doing anything substantive should be allowed to exist? The Government would do well to follow the example of private corporations, which face far more rigorous tests of performance. The number of such corporations has been almost unchanged during the past decade. Probably, the Government deserves commendation for preventing their "proliferation." But at the same time the question persists why it has been unable to cut the number significantly. The fact is that a public corporation, once it is established, rarely goes out of existence even if it has ceased to perform its original functions. Moreover, special corporations provide cozy places of employment for retired high Government officials. Naturally, pressures against closing such attractive routes to highly paid corporate posts are strong, but they should be firmly resisted.

Any experience with Japanese public corporations is likely to substantiate this view. However, it is also quite possible that public corporations in general, and Japanese public corporations in particular, may actually be useful tools in the fight against governmental bureaucratism.

Bureaucratism is the bane of the modern state—and of all very large social organizations. Bureaucracy itself is virtually unavoidable: a bureaucratically organized state, as Max Weber has shown, is the most rational way for people joined together in a large social system to ensure self-government, self-support, and self-defense. "In a modern

141

state the actual ruler is necessarily and unavoidably the bureaucracy, since power is exercised neither through parliamentary speeches nor monarchical enunciations but through the routines of administration." [1] Thus our concern should be not with the existence of the state and its bureaucratic apparatus, but with how to avoid or mitigate the evils of bureaucratism—its proliferation, lack of accountability, ineffectiveness, high cost, and devotion to the interests of the organization itself rather than to those who are ruled by it or those who pay for it.

In the West, recognizing and scrutinizing the problems of bureaucracy is a relatively recent tradition in political analysis. Most specialists in governmental administration regard Max Weber's early twentieth century theory of bureaucracy as "classical." [2] In contrast, the Sinitic civilizations of eastern Asia have perhaps twenty centuries more experience with bureaucracy than Western societies; their classical texts on the subject date from the first century B.C. Huan K'uan's *Yen-t'ieh lun* (Discourses on Salt and Iron) of 81 B.C. is an early compilation of ideas on the welfare state and the bureaucratic requirements for implementing it. Some Japanese commentators on the *Yen-t'ieh lun* hold Huan K'uan to be the patron saint of bureaucrats. Nagano Akira, for example, derives the following characteristics of bureaucrats from the *Yen-t'ieh lun*: (1) evasion of responsibility (because a bureaucrat's first thought is for the security of his own position, he cannot afford to do anything that might threaten that position), (2) passive resistance, (3) self-importance, (4) lack of foresight, (5) adaptation to the trend of events, (6) lack of self-reflection (passing responsibility to others for all mistaken policies), (7) willingness to do anything to get ahead, regardless of other loyalties, (8) selfishness, and (9) devotion to extravagance (expense accounts, luxury, travel, and so forth). [3] From the time of Huan K'uan to the present, the people of northeast Asia have been more familiar with and more self-conscious about the strengths and drawbacks of bureaucratic organization than have most other civilizations. [4]

---

[1] Max Weber, *Economy and Society*, Guenther Roth and Claus Wittich, eds. (New York: Bedminster Press, 1968), vol. 3, p. 1393.

[2] Dennis Wrong, ed., *Max Weber* (Englewood Cliffs, N.J.: Prentice-Hall, 1970), p. 141.

[3] Nagano Akira, *Kanryō* [Bureaucrats] (Tokyo: Seikai Kōron Sha, 1971), pp. 189-203. On the *Yen-t'ieh lun*, see Esson M. Gale, trans., *Discourses on Salt and Iron: A Debate on State Control of Commerce and Industry in Ancient China* (Leiden: E. J. Brill, 1931).

[4] For an excellent essay on the bureaucratic heritage in Japan from Tokugawa times to the present, see Najita Tetsuo, *Japan* (Englewood Cliffs, N.J.: Prentice-Hall, 1974).

Japan's Bureaucratic Heritage

Japan has a problem with bureaucracy. The modern Japanese state began under an oligarchy, which created and nurtured a powerful bureaucracy to serve its own interests; the common Western device for supervising the state, a parliamentary assembly of representatives of the people, has not yet developed to the point of real effectiveness in Japan. Weber commented that "the level of parliament depends on whether it does not merely discuss great issues but decisively influences them; in other words, its quality depends on whether what happens there matters, or whether parliament is nothing but the unwillingly tolerated rubber stamp of a ruling bureaucracy." Weighed by this standard, the postwar Japanese Diet must be found wanting.[5]

The American occupation sought to bolster the Diet, but the unintended effect of the sum of occupation reforms was to strengthen the state bureaucracy instead. As Maeda notes, many scholars in Japan regard the American policy of breaking up the zaibatsu as having been dictated by a desire on the part of American monopoly capital to weaken its Japanese competitors. In any case, the zaibatsu's dissolution had the effect of reinforcing state control over the economy.[6]

Despite its heritage of strong governmental control and the postwar resurgence of the state bureaucracy, Japan nevertheless does not suffer from the worst excesses of bureaucratism. Instead, it has had a talented and generally respected state administration. How is this anomaly to be explained? Part of the answer lies in Japan's long experience with bureaucracy, its informal norms for dealing with it, the traditions and the high prestige of the bureaucrats themselves, and the existence of potent, if not omnipotent, competitors to the bureaucracy in the political and industrial worlds. Another factor, one that has been largely unexplored, is Japan's state institutions—including the public corporations described in this book.

For example, although about half of the chief executive officers of Japan's public corporations are ex-bureaucrats, the other half are civilians; this mixture of bureaucrats and businessmen is itself a check on bureaucratic excesses. Moreover, the corporations must conform to commercial accounting rules, and the functions and powers of each company are spelled out in one or more laws, which makes them more

---

[5] Weber, *Economy and Society*, p. 1392. On the Diet and bureaucracy, see Chalmers Johnson, "Japan: Who Governs?" *The Journal of Japanese Studies*, vol. 2, no. 1 (Autumn 1975), pp. 1-28.

[6] Maeda Yasuyuki, "Tsūshō sangyō seisaku no rekishi-teki tenkai" [The historical development of trade and industrial policy], *Tsūsan jyānaru*, May 25, 1975, pp. 10-11.

accessible than official government agencies to scrutiny by the citizenry or the Diet. Organizational failure in a public corporation does not have the economic consequences for management that failure in a private corporation does, but it is easier to perceive than failure in an official department or bureau. The public corporation does not do away with the bureaucrat's classical tool of secrecy for defending himself, but it weakens it.

Financial Benefits

The fact that public corporations pay their own way, at least in principle, provides Japan with another major trade-off: reduced taxes. Despite the size and power of their bureaucracy, the Japanese enjoy the lowest tax rates of any OECD (Organization for Economic Cooperation and Development) nation. Table 11 compares combined national and local taxes as a percent of national income in the six leading industrial democracies. In 1974, the total tax burden for Japan was 21.1 percent of GNP, whereas for the United States it was 29.4 percent, England 36.4 percent, West Germany 31.3 percent, and Sweden 44.7 percent.[7]

Needless to say, the Japanese government provides fewer services than these other countries do. But lighter taxes also have contributed to Japan's political stability and social cohesion. As Randall Bartlett notes, "For any given bundle of expenditures, the tax program which presents the least visible taxes will be the vote maximizing one."[8] Not only does Japan have comparatively low taxes, but most of them are relatively invisible, taking the form of fees charged by the public corporations for their services. This feature may help to explain the Liberal Democratic Party's longevity as the dominant political force in the country, as well as the extraordinary political stability Japan has enjoyed since the war.

Whereas other advanced countries redistribute substantial portions of their citizens' incomes through taxes, the Japanese government concentrates instead on inducing people to spend their money themselves in ways that serve national policies. Nowhere is this clearer than in the social security and welfare systems. Japan has much weaker retirement and disability compensation systems than comparably industrialized nations; but it also has the highest rate of savings from personal disposable income of any society. Andrea Boltho explains this trade-off not

---

[7] *Shūkan asahi*, April 1, 1977, p. 33.
[8] Randall Bartlett, *Economic Foundations of Political Power* (New York: Free Press, 1973), pp. 94-95.

Table 11
COMPARATIVE TAX BURDENS IN SIX LEADING
INDUSTRIAL DEMOCRACIES

National and Local Taxes as Percent of National Income

Year	Japan[a]	U.S.	England	W. Germany	France	Italy
1968	18.4	29.1	38.6	29.2	26.7	24.6
1969	19.1	30.3	41.6	31.6	28.5	23.7
1970	19.5	29.1	42.5	29.3	27.6	23.5

[a] Japan is fiscal year (April to March); others are calendar years.
Source: Fukushima Ryōichi, Yamaguchi Mitsuhide, and Ishikawa Itaru, *Zaisei tōyūshi* [Fiscal investment and loan funds] (Tokyo: Ōkura Zaimu Kyōkai, 1973), p. 74.

in terms of any culturally based propensity to save, but rather in terms of the society's institutions:

The intentional or unintentional insufficiency of social security provisions was . . . one of the factors making for high savings. The intentional or unintentional lack of a capital market meant that the bulk of such private savings had to find their way into relatively liquid deposits held with either private or public financial institutions. In the latter case [that is, the case of the institutions that feed the FILP], the government could use the funds directly for investment in industrial infrastructure or for re-lending to private business. In the former case, the banking system [under the supervision of the Ministry of Finance and the Bank of Japan] would channel private savings to corporations.[9]

Thus, the Japanese government forces people to save by providing fewer services than other states, and then makes it easy for them to do so by taxing them lightly and providing government institutions in which they can keep their savings. The general economic culture also supports this system by paying employees relatively low monthly salaries but large (and eminently depositable) semiannual bonuses.

The Fiscal Investment and Loan Plan is the financial key to the growth of the public corporate sector, and the public corporate sector contributes to the health of the plan by relieving pressure from the public to expand the general account budget. The availability of the

[9] Andrea Boltho, *Japan, An Economic Survey 1953–1973* (London: Oxford University Press, 1975), p. 127.

FILP as a separate investment budget also has given the Japanese government a counter-cyclical fiscal capacity despite its long-standing post-occupation commitment to balanced budgets. As in most other countries, using funds from the FILP for fiscal policy purposes has been most effective for helping to pull the economy out of recession, seldom for dampening down a boom. The figures in table 12 reveal heavy counter-cyclical expenditure plans in 1964–1965 and in 1971–1972, both periods of recession or serious economic uncertainty.

Advantages in Weakness

Given the impressive performance of the Japanese economy in the post-war world, the problem for analysts is to explain the unusual capabilities of Japanese governmental institutions, not their limitations. Even their deficiencies, however, may have features that work against bureaucratism. For example, *amakudari* is caused by early retirement; and forcing all bureaucrats out of their sinecures by age fifty-five inhibits the tendency of life-long bureaucrats to become rigid and complacent. It also puts them on notice that they must eventually enter and perform in a world that is much less tolerant of the arrogance and the legalistic

Table 12
GROWTH RATES OF GNP AND OF THE FILP
(percent)

Year	GNP	FILP
1964	15.9	20.8
1965	10.6	20.9
1966	17.2	25.1
1967	17.9	17.8
1968	17.8	13.0
1969	18.0	14.0
1970	16.3	16.3
1971	10.7	19.6
1972	17.4	31.6

Note: FILP is planned, not supplemental, expenditures.
Source: Fukushima Ryōichi, Yamaguchi Mitsuhide, and Ishikawa Itaru, *Zaisei tōyūshi* [Fiscal investment and loan funds] (Tokyo: Ōkura Zaimu Kyōkai, 1973), p. 97.

mentality that often characterize bureaucrats. Further, the need to descend from heaven stimulates bureaucrats to learn new things throughout their active-duty service, which can be salutary, though it can also produce conflicts of interest.

Similarly, the tendency of public corporations to proliferate, due partly to the fact that bureaucrats who lack business talent must "side-slip" rather than descend, is not necessarily a bad thing. It can stimulate competition; as Richard E. Wagner observes:

> Competition among bureaus in a bureaucracy can have effects similar to competition among firms in an industry. If bureaus compete among themselves for the right to supply a sponsor, the demand curve faced by any one bureau becomes more elastic. Hence, the ability of the bureau to act as if it were a discriminating monopoly is reduced, thereby retarding the tendency toward excess supply. Currently, there may be substantial merit in creating a number of competing bureaus rather than in trying to consolidate bureaus. . . .One of the most promising areas of research in the public economy lies in examining the performance of alternative institutional frameworks for strengthening the operation of this unseen hand.[10]

In Japan, the intense competition among established ministries (between the Ministry of Finance and MITI, for example) is legendary, and it undoubtedly contributes to the performance and high esprit de corps of the elite bureaucrats. As extensions of the ministries, the public corporations perpetuate this competition, sometimes to the advantage of the public. Occasionally, however, competition has led to divided responsibilities and failure—the case of the ill-fated ship *Mutsu* and the Japan Nuclear Ship Development Agency (a *jigyōdan* jointly controlled by MITI, the Science and Technology Agency, and the Ministry of Transportation) is an instance. Advantageous competition among bureaucracies and their extensions may be impossible to institutionalize; but the mere presence of large numbers and overlapping jurisdictions is not in itself a sign of bureaucratism.

Official bureaucracy is the major growth enterprise of the contemporary world. An unintended consequence of virtually every proposed solution to the various problems of the advanced industrial democracies—depletion of resources, technological innovation, environmental protection, and so forth—is more official bureaucracy. This growth is inevitable, given the risks and the size of the investments needed to implement any solutions to such pervasive problems. Japan

---

[10] Richard E. Wagner, *The Public Economy* (Chicago: Markham, 1973), pp. 122-23.

and societies like it, with their greater experience of and alertness to the evils of bureaucratism, may well outperform societies like the United States, in which there is no natural resistance to bureaucratism. The extensive use of public corporations is part of the secret of how Japan has successfully used official bureaucracy and at the same time kept under control its counterproductive manifestations.

Appendix

JAPAN'S SPECIAL LEGAL ENTITIES
(TOKUSHU HŌJIN) AS OF APRIL 1975

The type of corporation is indicated by the last term of the Japanese title. All *kabushiki kaisha* (K.K.) are "special companies" (*tokushu kaisha*). All *ginkō* are "special banks" (*tokushu ginkō*).

English titles of corporations are those listed in *Kenkyūsha's New Japanese-English Dictionary*, 4th ed. (Tokyo, 1974), pp. 2099–2100.

The numbers of corporations created each year do not agree with table 4 in chapter 2 because that table records the year of Diet authorization and this table records the year of actual establishment.

KEY TO ABBREVIATIONS FOR CONTROLLING
MINISTRIES AND AGENCIES

BOT	Board of Trade Bōeki-chō	MOE	Ministry of Education Mombu-shō
EA	Environment Agency Kankyō-chō	MOF	Ministry of Finance Ōkura-shō
EPA	Economic Planning Agency Keizai Kikaku-chō	MOL	Ministry of Labor Rōdō-shō
HDA	Hokkaido Development Agency Hokkaidō Kaihatsu-chō	MOP	Ministry of Posts and Telecommunications Yūsei-shō
MAF	Ministry of Agriculture and Forestry Nōrin-shō	MOT	Ministry of Transportation Un'yu-shō
		MOW	Ministry of Welfare Kōsei-shō
MCI	Ministry of Commerce and Industry Shōkō-shō	NLA	National Land Agency Kokudo-chō
MFA	Ministry of Foreign Affairs Gaimu-shō	ODA	Okinawa Development Agency Okinawa Kaihatsu-chō
MHA	Ministry of Home Affairs Jichi-shō	PB	Price Board Bukka-chō
MITI	Ministry of International Trade and Industry Tsūshō Sangyō-shō	PMO	Prime Minister's Office Sōri-fu
MOC	Ministry of Construction Kensetsu-shō	STA	Science and Technology Agency Kagaku Gijutsu-chō

149

JAPAN'S SPECIAL LEGAL ENTITIES (TOKUSHU HŌJIN) AS OF APRIL 1975

Name	Percent of Fixed Capital Supplied by Government	Control	Direct Access to FILP	Number of Employees (as of April 1975, unless otherwise noted) and Remarks
1923				
Central Cooperative Bank for Agriculture and Forestry (Nōrin Chūō Kinko)	0	MOF MAF	No	2,771
1936				
Bank for Commerce and Industrial Cooperatives (Shōkō Kumiai Chūō Kinko)	62.5	MOF MITI	Yes	6,327
Tōhoku Industrial Company (Tōhoku Kōgyō K.K.)	99.0	EPA NLA	Yes	806. Reorganized in 1957 as Tōhoku District Development Co.
1939				
Imperial Mining Development Company (Teikoku Kōgyō Kaihatsu K.K.)	0	MCI MITI	No	Broken up by SCAP April 1, 1950. In receivership until abolished in 1970.
1941				
Teito Rapid Transit Authority (Teito Kōsokudo Kōtsū Eidan)	0	MOC MOT	Yes	10,044
1944				
Japan Scholarship Foundation (Nihon Ikuei Kai)	50.0	MOE	No	589. Fifty percent of capital supplied by Imperial Household.

150

1947

Name				
Liquor Distribution Kōdan (Shurui Haikyū Kōdan)	100	MOF	No	3,654 (on 4/26/48). In existence 12/12/47–7/1/49.
Fertilizer Distribution Kōdan (Hiryō Haikyū Kōdan)	100	MAF	No	4,641 (on 4/26/48). In existence 6/20/47–8/1/50.
Fodder Distribution Kōdan (Shiryō Haikyū Kōdan)	100	MAF	No	549 (on 4/26/48). In existence 12/17/47–4/1/50.
Staple Food Distribution Kōdan (Shokuryō Haikyū Kōdan)	100	MAF	No	84,954 (on 4/26/48). In existence 12/30/47–4/12/51.
Grocery Distribution Kōdan (Shokuryōhin Haikyū Kōdan)	100	MAF	No	3,199 (on 4/26/48). In existence 12/27/47–3/31/50. Merged to create Sugar and Oil Distribution Kōdan, which lasted until 3/31/51.
Oil and Fats Distribution Kōdan (Yuryō Haiykū Kōdan)	100	MAF MCI MITI	No	524 (on 4/26/48). In existence 12/17/47–3/31/51. Same as Grocery Distribution Kōdan.
Coal Distribution Kōdan (Haitan Kōdan)	100	MCI MITI	No	12,799 (on 4/26/48). In existence 4/17/47–9/15/49.
Petroleum Distribution Kōdan (Sekiyu Haikyū Kōdan)	100	MCI	No	3,144 (on 4/26/48). In existence 4/15/47–3/31/49.
Industrial Recovery Kōdan (Sangyō Fukkō Kōdan)	100	MCI MITI	No	512 (on 4/26/48). In existence 4/15/47–3/31/51.
Mining and Manufactured Goods Trade Kōdan (Kōkōhin Bōeki Kōdan)	100	BOT MITI	No	2,749 (on 4/26/48). In existence 4/17/47–1/31/51.
Textiles Trade Kōdan (Sen'i Bōeki Kōdan)	100	BOT MITI	No	2,374 (on 4/26/48). In existence 4/17/47–12/31/50.

Appendix (continued)

Name	Percent of Fixed Capital Supplied by Government	Control	Direct Access to FILP	Number of Employees (as of April 1975, unless otherwise noted) and Remarks
Foodstuffs Trade Kōdan (Shokuryō Bōeki Kōdan)	100	BOT	No	1,429 (on 4/26/48). In existence 4/17/47–3/31/49.
Raw Materials Trade Kōdan (Genzairyō Bōeki Kōdan)	100	BOT	No	683 (on 4/26/48). In existence 4/17/47–3/31/49.
Shipbuilding Kōdan (Sempaku Kōdan)	100	MCI MITI	No	146 (on 4/26/48). In existence 4/17/47–7/1/49.
Prince Adjustment Kōdan (Kakaku Chōsei Kōdan)	100	PB	No	1,168 (on 4/26/48). In existence 4/15/47–3/31/51.
1948				
Social Insurance Medical Fee Payment Fund (Shakai Hoken Shinnyō Hōshū Shiharai Kikin)	40.0	MOW	No	4,672
1949				
Japan Monopoly Corporation (Nihon Sembai Kōsha)	100	MOF	No	41,097
Japan National Railways (Nihon Kokuyū Tetsudō)	100	MOT	Yes	432,000
People's Finance Corporation (Kokumin Kin'yū Kōko)	100	MOF	Yes	4,458

1950				
Housing Loan Corporation (Jūtaku Kin'yū Kōko)	100	MOC MOF	Yes	1,129
Japan Export-Import Bank (Nihon Yushutsunyū Ginkō)	100	MOF	Yes	442
Japan Broadcasting Corporation (Nihon Hōsō Kyōkai)	0	MOP	No	16,441
1951				
Japan Development Bank (Nihon Kaihatsu Ginkō)	100	MOF	Yes	1,055
1952				
Private School Development Association (Shiritsu Gakkō Shinkōkai)	100	MOE	Yes	Abolished 1970.
Nippon Telegraph and Telephone Public Corporation (Nihon Denshin Denwa Kōsha)	100	MOP	Yes	308,341
Electric Power Development Company (Dengen Kaihatsu K.K.)	74.0	MITI	Yes	2,689
1953				
Kokusai Denshin Denwa Company (International Telegraph and Telephone Co.)	100	MOP	No	5,738
Japan Air Lines Company, Ltd. (Nihon Kōkū K.K.)	45.0	MOT	No	20,522
Agriculture, Forestry, and Fishery Finance Corporation (Nōringyogyō Kin'yū Kōko)	100	MOF MAF	Yes	942

Appendix (continued)

Name	Percent of Fixed Capital Supplied by Government	Control	Direct Access to FILP	Number of Employees (as of April 1975, unless otherwise noted) and Remarks
Smaller Business Finance Corporation (Chūshō Kigyō Kin'yū Kōko)	100	MOF MITI	Yes	1,720
1954				
Japan Ammonium Sulfate Export Company (Nihon Ryūan Yushutsu K.K.)	0	MITI	No	29
Private School Personnel Mutual Aid Association (Shiritsu Gakkō Kyōshokuin Kyōsai Kumiai)	0	MOE	No	224
Foundation for Promoting Social Welfare Agencies, Inc. (Shakai Fukushi Jigyō Shinkōkai)	100	MOW	Yes	58
Japan [Horse] Racing Association (Nihon Chūō Keiba Kai)	100	MAF	No	1,790
1955				
Agricultural Land Development Machinery Public Corporation (Nōchi Kaihatsu Kikai Kōdan)	100	MAF	Yes	552. In 1974 changed to Agricultural Land Development Corp.
Aichi Prefecture Water Resources Corporation (Aichi Yōsui Kōdan)	100	MAF	Yes	Abolished 1968.
Japan Housing Corporation (Nihon Jūtaku Kōdan)	97.5	MOC	Yes	5,064

Name	%	Ministry		Notes
Coal Mining Facilities Corporation (Sekitan Kōgyō Seibi Jigyōdan)	100	MITI	No	In 1960 changed to Rationalization of Coal Industry Corp.
Petroleum Resources Development Company (Sekiyu Shigen Kaihatsu K.K.)	100	MITI	No	In 1967 changed to Japan Petroleum Development Corp. and upgraded to a *kōdan*.
Japan Overseas Emigration Promotion Company (Nihon Kaigai Ijū Shinkō K.K.)	100	MFA	No	In 1963 changed to Japan Emigration Service and upgraded to a *jigyōdan*.
Japan School Lunch Society (Nihon Gakkō Kyūshoku Kai)	0	MOE	No	39
Amami Guntō Promotion Credit Fund (Amami Guntō Shinkō Kaihatsu Kikin)	89.6	MOF MHA NLA	No	29
1956				
Nuclear Fuel Public Corporation (Genshi Nenyrō Kōsha)	100	STA	Yes	In 1967 changed to Power Reactor and Nuclear Fuel Development Corp. and downgraded to a *jigyōdan*.
Forest Development Corporation (Shinrin Kaihatsu Kōdan)	100	MAF	Yes	493
Japan Highway Public Corporation (Nihon Dōro Kōdan)	100	MOC	Yes	7,255
Hokkaido and Tōhoku Development Corporation (Hokkaidō Tōhoku Kaihatsu Kōko)	100	HDA MOF NLA	Yes	286
Japan Atomic Energy Research Institute (Nihon Genshiryoku Kenkyū-jo)	98.1	STA	No	2,179

Appendix (continued)

Name	Percent of Fixed Capital Supplied by Government	Control	Direct Access to FILP	Number of Employees (as of April 1975, unless otherwise noted) and Remarks
Mutual Aid Fund for Compensation for Accidents on Duty of Firemen and Others (Shōbōdan'inra Kōmu Saigai Hoshōra Kyōsai Kikin)	0	MHA	No	24
1957				
Tōhoku District Development Company (Tōhoku Kaihatsu K.K.)	99.0	EPA NLA	Yes	806
Labor Welfare Corporation (Rōdō Fukushi Jigyōdan)	100	MOL	Yes	8,607
Finance Corporation for Local Public Enterprises (Kōei Kigyō Kin'yū Kōko)	100	MOF MHA	Yes	79
Nampō Brethren Relief Association (Nampō Dōhō Engokai)	0	PMO	No	Abolished 1972.
Japan Information Center of Science and Technology (Nihon Kagaku Gijutsu Jōhō Sentā)	99.3	STA	No	329
Japan Keirin [Bicycle Racing] Association (Nihon Jitensha Shinkōkai)	0	MITI	No	335
1958				
Smaller Business Credit Insurance Corporation (Chūshō Kigyō Shin'yō Hoken Kōko)	100	MOF MITI	No	399

Japan Silk Export Storage Company (Nihon Yushutsu Kiito Hokan K.K.)	37.5	MAF	No	Abolished 1966.
Hokkaidō Underground Resources Development Company (Hokkaidō Chika Shigen Kaihatsu K.K.)	90	MITI	No	Abolished 1968.
Institute of Physical and Chemical Research (Rikagaku Kenkyū-jo)	97.3	STA	No	618
National Stadium (Kokuritsu Kyōgijō)	100	MOE	No	212
Japan External Trade Organization (JETRO) (Nihon Bōeki Shinkōkai)	100	MITI	No	614
Postal Savings Fund Raising Management Association (Yūbin Bokin Kanrikai)	0	MOP	No	Abolished 1968.
Japan Institute of Labor (Nihon Rōdō Kyōkai)	100	MOL	No	58
1959				
Agriculture, Forestry, and Fisheries Organizations Employees Mutual Aid Association (Nōringyogyō Dantai Shokuin Kyōsai Kumiai)	0	MAF	No	205
Internal Passenger Ship Corporation (Kokunai Ryokakusen Kōdan)	100	MOT	Yes	95. In 1961 changed to Designated Shipping Credit Corp., in 1966 to Maritime Credit Corp., both *kōdan*.
Tokyo Expressway Public Corporation (Shuto Kōsoku Dōro Kōdan)	50.0	MOC	Yes	1,404

Appendix (continued)

Name	Percent of Fixed Capital Supplied by Government	Control	Direct Access to FILP	Number of Employees (as of April 1975, unless otherwise noted) and Remarks
Japan Silkworm and Cocoon Corporation (Nihon Sanken Jigyōdan)	100	MAF	No	In 1966 merged with Japan Silk Export Storage Co., a *tokushu kaisha*, to become Japan Raw Silk Corp.
Smaller Enterprise Retirement Allowance Mutual Aid Projects Corporation (Chūshō Kigyō Taishokukin Kyōsai Jigyōdan)	0	MOL	No	234
Nippon Aeroplane Manufacturing Company (Nihon Kōkūki Seizō K.K.)	53.8	MITI	No	103
Japan Sugar Beet Improvement Foundation (Nihon Tensai Shinkōkai)	100	MAF	No	52. Abolished 1973.
Japan National Tourist Organization (Kokusai Kankō Shinkōkai)	100	MOT	No	112. Name changed in 1964.
1960				
Japan School Safety Association (Nihon Gakkō Anzen Kai)	0	MOE	No	257
Medical Care Facilities Finance Corporation (Iryō Kin'yū Kōko)	100	MOF MOW	Yes	177
Fishermen's Cooperative Associations Equipment Fund (Gyogyō Kyōdō Kumiai Seibi Kikin)	50.0	MAF	No	Abolished 1972.

158

Name				
Institute of Asian Economic Affairs (Ajia Keizai Kenkyū-jo)	87.4	MITI	No	247. Also known as Institute of Developing Economies.
Rationalization of Coal Industry Corporation (Sekitan Kōgyō Gōrika Jigyōdan)	100	MITI	No	254
1961				
Overseas Economic Cooperation Fund (Kaigai Keizai Kyōryoku Kikin)	100	EPA	Yes	156
Research Development Corporation of Japan (Shingijutsu Kaihatsu Jigyōdan)	100	STA	No	66
Pension Welfare Service Public Corporation (Nenkin Fukushi Jigyōdan)	0	MOW	Yes	139
Livestock Industry Promotion Corporation (Chikusan Shinkō Jigyōdan)	94.1	MAF	No	103
Employment Promotion Projects Corporation (Koyō Sokushin Jigyōdan)	99.6	MOL	Yes	4,453
Northern Territories Association (Hoppō Kyōkai)	100	PMO	No	In 1969 changed to Northern Territories Policy Assn.
Fish Price Stabilization Fund (Gyoka Antei Kikin)	48.8	MAF	No	Abolished 1968.
1962				
Water Resources Development Public Corporation (Suishigen Kaihatsu Kōdan)	100	MOC NLA	Yes	1,987
Hanshin Superhighway Corporation (Hanshin Kōsoku Dōro Kōdan)	50.0	MOC	Yes	852

Appendix (continued)

Name	Percent of Fixed Capital Supplied by Government	Control	Direct Access to FILP	Number of Employees (as of April 1975, unless otherwise noted) and Remarks
Overseas Technical Cooperation Agency (Kaigai Gitjutsu Kyōryoku Jigyōdan)	100	MFA	No	433. In 1974, absorbed into International Cooperation Agency, a *jigyōdan*.
Coal Mine Area Rehabilitation Corporation (Santan Chiiki Shinkō Jigyōdan)	100	MITI	Yes	In 1972 changed to Industrial Relocation and Coal Production Areas Promotion Corp., a *kōdan*, and in 1974 to Regional Promotion and Facilities Corp.
Post Office Life Insurance and Annuities Welfare Corporation (Kan'i Hoken Yūbin Nenkin Fukushi Jigyōdan)	92.1	MOP	No	2,337
Better Living Research Institute (Kokumin Seikatsu Kenkyū-jo)	67.1	EPA	No	In 1970 reorganized as Better Living Information Center.
Institute of Agricultural Machinery (Nōrin Kikaika Kenkyū-jo)	93.6	MAF	No	89
Japan Local Racing Association (Chihō Keiba Zenkoku Kyōkai)	0	MAF	No	203
Japan Small Automobile Promotion Association (Nihon Kogata Jidōsha Shinkōkai)	0	MITI	No	75
Japan Shipbuilding Industry Foundation (Nihon Senpaku Shinkōkai)	0	MOT	No	58

1963

Organization	%	Ministry		Notes
Japan Nuclear Ship Development Agency (Nihon Genshiryokusen Kaihatsu Jigyōdan)	90.3	STA MOT	No	130
Japan Emigration Service (Kaigai Ijū Jigyōdan)	100	MFA	No	437. Replaced Japan Overseas Emigration Promotion Co. of 1955. In 1974 absorbed into International Cooperation Agency.
Metallic Minerals Prospecting Finance Corporation (Kinzoku Kōbutsu Tankō Yūshi Jigyōdan)	100	MITI	Yes	159. Name changed in 1964 and 1973.
Coal for Electric Power Distribution Company (Denryoku Yōtan Hambai K.K.)	37.5	MITI	No	32. Name changed in 1965.
Tokyo Small Business Investment Company (Tōkyō Chūshō Kigyō Tōshi Ikusei K.K.)	4.0	MITI	No	51
Nagoya Small Business Investment Company (Nagoya Chūshō Kigyō Tōshi Ikusei K.K.)	8.0	MITI	No	32
Osaka Small Business Investment Company (Ōsaka Chūshō Kigyō Tōshi Ikusei K.K.)	3.25	MITI	No	42
Forestry Credit Fund (Ringyō Shin'yō Kikin)	27.1	MAF	No	46
Mine Damage Compensation Fund (Kōgai Baishō Kikin)	100	MITI	No	389. Name changed in 1965. In 1968 upgraded to a jigyōdan.
Institute for Safety of High Pressure Gas Engineering (Kōatsu Gasu Hoan Kyōkai)	0	MITI	No	58
Japan Medium and Small Enterprises Guidance Center (Nihon Chūshō Kigyō Shidō Sentā)	100	MITI	No	Abolished 1967.

161

Appendix (continued)

Name	Percent of Fixed Capital Supplied by Government	Control	Direct Access to FILP	Number of Employees (as of April 1975, unless otherwise noted) and Remarks
Japan Fire Equipment Inspection Council (Nihon Shōbō Kentei Kyōkai)	100	MHA	No	91
1964				
Japan Railway Construction Corporation (Nihon Tetsudō Kensetu Kōdan)	73.3	MOT	Yes	3,350
National Education Center (Kokuritsu Kyōiku Kaikan)	100	MOE	No	79
Fisheries Mutual Aid Fund (Gyogyō Kyōsai Kikin)	44.1	MAF	No	5
Japan Electric Meters Inspection Corporation (Nihon Denki Keiki Kentei-jo)	74.1	MITI	No	1,211
Construction Industry Retirement Allowance Mutual Aid Association (Kensetsugyō Taishoku Kyōsai Kumiai)	0	MOL	No	54
Mutual Aid Association for Personnel of Regional Organizations (Chihō Dantai Kankei Dantai Shokuin Kyōsai Kumiai)	0	MHA	No	14
1965				
Social Development Research Institute (Shakai Hoshō Kenkyū-jo)	0	MOW	No	22

Name	%	Ministry	Subsidiary	No.	Notes
Public Nuisances Prevention Corporation (Kōgai Bōshi Jigyōdan)	100	MOW MITI EA	Yes	124	
Hachirōgata [Akita Prefecture] New Community Development Corporation (Hachirōgata Shinnōson Kensetsu Jigyōdan)	100	MAF	Yes	223	
Japan Sugar Price Stabilization Agency (Tōka Antei Jigyōdan)	0	MAF	No	99	
Smaller Enterprises Mutual Relief Corporation (Shōkibo Kigyō Kyōsai Jigyōdan)	100	MITI	No	81	
Japan Automobile Terminal Company (Nihon Jidōsha Tāminaru K.K.)	29.0	MOT	No	82	
Olympic Memorial Youth Center (Orinpikku Kinen Seishōnen Sōgō Sentā)	100	MOE	No	81	
1966					
Japan Raw Silk Corporation (Nihon Sanshi Jigyōdan)	83.4	MAF	No	780	32. Replaces Japan Silkworm and Cocoon Corp., 1959, Japan Silk Export Storage Co., 1958.
New Tokyo International Airport Corporation (Shin Tōkyō Kokusai Kūkō Kōdan)	100	MOT	Yes	193	
National Theater (Kokuritsu Gekijō)	100	MOE	No	48	
Association of Children's Land (Kodomo no Kuni Kyōkai)	100	MOW	No	47	
1967					
Japan Workers' Housing Association (Nihon Kinrōsha Jūtaku Kyōkai)	0	MOC	No		

Appendix (continued)

Name	Percent of Fixed Capital Supplied by Government	Control	Direct Access to FILP	Number of Employees (as of April 1975, unless otherwise noted) and Remarks
Japan Petroleum Development Corporation (Sekiyu Kaihatsu Kōdan)	100	MITI	Yes	177. Replaces Petroleum Development Co. of 1955.
Keihin Port Development Authority (Keihin Gaibō Futō Kōdan)	50.0	MOT	Yes	188. Tokyo Bay area.
Hanshin Port Development Authority (Hanshin Gaibō Futō Kōdan)	50.0	MOT	Yes	190. Osaka Bay area.
Power Reactor and Nuclear Fuel Development Corporation (Dōryokuro Kakunenryō Kaihatsu Jigyōdan)	94.7	STA	Yes	1,826. Replaces Nuclear Fuel kōsha of 1956.
Small Business Promotion Corporation (Chūshō Kigyō Shinkō Jigyōdan)	100	MITI	Yes	244. Replaces Japan Medium and Small Enterprises Guidance Center of 1963.
Environmental Sanitation Business Finance Corporation (Kankyō Eisei Kin'yū Kōko)	100	MOF MOW	Yes	56
Japan Society for the Promotion of Science (Nihon Gakujutsu Shinkōkai)	0	MOE	No	37
Sake Brewers' Retirement Allowance Mutual Aid Association (Seishu Seizōgyō Taishokukin Kyōsai Kumiai)	0	MOL	No	10

	%	Agency		Notes
1968				
Coal Mine Damage Corporation (Sekitan Kōgai Jigyōdan)	100	MITI	No	389. Replaces Mine Damage Compensation Fund of 1963.
1969				
Northern Territories Policy Association (Hoppō Ryōdo Mondai Taisaku Kyōkai)	100	PMO	No	19. Replaces Northern Territories Assn. of 1961.
National Space Development Agency (Uchū Kaihatsu Jigyōdan)	97.1	STA MOT	No	619
1970				
Better Living Information Center (Kokumin Seikatsu Sentā)	100	EPA	No	102. Replaces Better Living Research Inst. of 1962.
Japan Private School Promotion Foundation (Nihon Shigaku Shinkō Zaidan)	100	MOE	Yes	116. Replaces Private School Development Assn. of 1951.
Farmer Pension Fund (Nōgyōsha Nenkin Kikin)	0	MAF	No	79
Honshu-Shikoku Bridge Authority (Honshū-Shikoku Renrakukyō Kōdan)	71.6	MOT MOC	Yes	582
1971				
Association for Welfare of the Mentally and Physically Handicapped (Shinshin Shōgaisha Fukushi Kyōkai)	100	MOW	No	286
1972				
Okinawa Development Finance Corporation (Okinawa Shinkō Kaihatsu Kin'yū Kōko)	100	MOF ODA	Yes	215
Japan Foundation (Kokusai Kōryū Kikin)	99.9	MFA	No	109

Appendix (continued)

Name	Percent of Fixed Capital Supplied by Government	Control	Direct Access to FILP	Number of Employees (as of April 1975, unless otherwise noted) and Remarks
Industrial Relocation and Coal Production Areas Promotion Corporation (Kōgyō Saihaichi Santan Chiiki Shinkō Kōdan)	100	MITI	Yes	269. Replaces Coal Mine Area Rehabilitation Corp. of 1962. In 1974 renamed Regional Promotion and Facilities Corp.
Okinawa Electric Power Company (Okinawa Denryoku K.K.)	99.9	MITI	No	1,066
1974				
International Cooperation Agency (Kokusai Kyōryoku Jigyōdan)	100	MFA	No	994. Merges Overseas Technical Cooperation Agency of 1962 and Japan Emigration Service of 1963.
Agricultural Land Development Corporation (Nōyōchi Kaihatsu Kōdan)	100	MAF	Yes	587. Replaces Agricultural Land Development Machinery Corp. of 1955.
Regional Promotion and Facilities Corporation (Chiiki Shinkō Setsubi Kōdan)	100	MITI NLA MOC	Yes	515. Replaces Industrial Relocation and Coal Production Areas Promotion Corp. of 1972.
Pollution Health Damage Compensation Association (Kōgai Kenkō Higai Hoshō Kyōkai)	0	MITI	No	68

Index

Administrative guidance, 23, 126
Administrative Management Agency, 35f., 49, 55, 111, 138
Agriculture, Forestry, and Fishery Finance Corporation, 96
Aichi Prefecture Water Resources Corporation, 40, 98
Aiyukawa Gisuke, 68, 137
Ajia Keizai Kenkyū-jo, *see* Institute of Developing Economies
Akazawa Shōichi, 46f., 58
Alaska Pulp Company, 43, 58
Alcohol Monopoly Law, 32
Amakudari ("descent from heaven"), 16, 33, 41, 44, 49, 102-114, 139, 146-47; first use of term, 70; in oil industry, 127
Amaya Naohiro, 10, 58
Arabian Oil Company of Japan, 42, 56, 58, 109, 124
Arisawa Hiromi, 88, 130
Asano Cement Company, 72
Ashida Hitoshi, 30, 90*n*
Ashihara Yoshishige, 138
Asian Packaging Federation, 49
Asia Oil Company, 56-57

Bank for Commerce and Industrial Cooperatives, 43-44, 51, 96, 110f.
Bank of Japan, 88f., 91, 95, 110f., 145
Bank of Korea, 66, 85
Bank of Taiwan, 66, 85
Bartlett, Randall, 144
Battle Act, 53
Bisson, T. A., 72
Black, Cyril E., 17-21, 113
Board of Audit, 103

Board of Trade, 74
Boltho, Andrea, 18-19, 144-45
Brazil, 46; Japanese emigration to, 73*n*
Bridgestone Tire and Rubber Company, 55
Bureau of Legislation, 44
Burroughs computer company, 58
Buy America Act, 58

Cabinet Planning Board, 46, 70f., 73, 77
Caltex Oil Company, 56
Cement Control Association, 72
Central Cooperative Bank for Agriculture and Forestry, 43
Central Social Insurance and Medical Care Council, 2
China, 18, 36, 53, 64, 69, 120, 127, 133, 137; and Nishihara loans, 85; and bureaucracy, 142
Chōsei ("coordination"), 2, 33
Civil Code, 35, 49
Coal Agency, 74
Coal Distribution Kōdan, 78, 127
Coal for Electric Power Distribution Company, 123
Coal Mine Area Rehabilitation Corporation, 130f.
Coal Mine Damage Corporation, 112-13, 123, 128
Coal Mining Facilities Corporation, 128-29
Coal Mining Rationalization Special Measures Law, 128
Coal Special Account, 130f.
Commercial Code, 35
Communist Party of Japan, 52, 77

167

Morozumi Yoshihiko, 109, 139
Murase Naokai, 27, 44
Mutsu Ogawara Development Company, 48

Nagai Ryūtarō, 133
Nagano Akira, 142
Nagano Shigeo, 59, 73
Nakagawa Riichirō, 126
Nakai Reisaku, 67
Nakamura Tateki, 95
Nakano Yūrei, 114
Nakayama Sohei, 95
National Administration Organization Law, 2
National General Mobilization Law, 70, 76f.
National Hospitals Special Account, 48
National Land Agency, 131
National Personnel Authority, 103
National policy companies, 25, 27, 42, 44, 53-54, 66
National Public Service Law, 30-31, 103
National Public Service Mutual Aid Association Law, 108
National Space Development Agency, 34
NCR Computer Company, 58
Nettl, J. P., 12n, 61-62
New Japan Steel Company, 59-60, 109. See also Japan Iron and Steel Company; Yawata Iron and Steel Company
New Tokyo International Airport Corporation, 34
Nichi-nan Sangyō K.K., 73
Nihon Sekiyu K.K., 56
Nippon Aeroplane Manufacturing Company, 45-47, 54
Nippon Electric Company, 58
Nippon Hassōden, see Japan Electric Power Generation and Transmission Company
Nippon Kangyō Bank, 66, 70, 85, 95
Nippon Kōkan K.K., 67, 73
Nippon Mining Company, 56, 72
Nippon Soda Company, 114
Nippon Telegraph and Telephone Public Corporation, 29, 38, 96
Nishihara Kamezō, 85
Nissan Automobile Company, 59
Northern Territories Policy Association, 47
North Sumatra Petroleum Development Company, 56, 124
N.Y.K. Line, 54

Ōbori Hiromu, 139
Odahashi Sadaju, 22-23
OECD, see Organization for Economic Cooperation and Development
Ojima Arakazu, 60n
Ōjimi Yoshihisa, 109, 125n
Oki Electric Company, 58
Okinawa Development Agency, 42
Okinawa Development Finance Corporation, 42
Okinawa Electric Power Company, 45
Ōno Bamboku, 90n, 138
Organization for Economic Cooperation and Development, 15, 18, 34, 58, 144
Organization of Petroleum Exporting Countries (OPEC), 119
Oriental Development Company, 66
Osaka Shōsen, 54
Ōta Kaoru, 50
Ōta Risaburō, 95
Overseas Trade Promotion Association, 51
Ōwada Teiji, 114

Patent Attorneys' Association of Japan, 49
Patrick, Hugh, 17-18
People's Finance Corporation, 96, 111
Petroleum Cooperative Sales Company, 69
Petroleum Distribution Kōdan, 125
Petroleum Industry Law, 56, 126
Petroleum policy, 22, 55-57, 123-27
Petroleum Resources Development Company, 54, 56, 124-25
Petroleum Resources Development Law, 123
Planning, 17, 21-22, 65 and n, 78
Postal savings, see Fiscal Investment and Loan Plan
Post Office Life Insurance and Annuities Welfare Corporation, 41
Power Reactor and Nuclear Fuel Development Corporation, 26, 123, 138
Price Agency, 78
Price Control Ordinance, 72
Prime Minister's Office, 35, 47, 112
Prince Motors Company, 59
Public Corporations and National Enterprises Labor Relations Law, 30-31, 38
Public Utilities Commission, 135-36

Rationalization of Coal Industry Corporation, 123, 129

171

United States, 52f., 55-56, 63; and bureaucratism, 14, 148; aid to Japan, 18, 92-93; Department of Defense, 23; Department of Commerce, 23; surplus agricultural commodities, 40, 98, 137; Mutual Security Administration, 46.
   See also Supreme Commander for the Allied Powers
Univac Computer Company, 58
Urabe Toshio, 53
Utsumi Kiyoharu, 137

Wagner, Richard E., 147
Watanabe Tsunehiko, 21
Watanabe Yōzō, 55
Weber, Max, 141-43
Whitney, Gen. Courtney, 93
World Bank, *see* International Bank for Reconstruction and Development

Yalu River Extraction and Lumber Company, 53, 66
Yamamoto Shigenobu, 59, 109
Yamashita Tarō, 42
Yatabe Akira, 95
Yawata Iron and Steel Company, 20, 59, 67, 73f.
Yokkaichi, 32, 42, 125
Yokohama Rubber Company, 55
Yokohama Specie Bank, 85
Yokoo Shigemi, 136
Yokoyama Michio, 138
Yoshida Shigeru, 77, 88, 95, 135
Yoshimitsu Hisashi, 59
Yoshimura Seizō, 138
Yoshino Shinji, 68
Yoshitake Kiyohiko, 108
Yūdō ("inducement"), 21-22, 99

Zen Keinosuke, 77